INTENSITY WITH INTEGRITY

KEITH BROWN

INTENSITY WITH INTEGRITY

Keith Brown, Intensity with Integrity

ISBN 1-887002-42-1

Cross Training Publishing
1604 S. Harrison St.
Grand Island, NE 68803
(308) 384-5762

This book is manufactured in the United States of America.

Library of Congress Cataloging in Publication Data in Progress.

Published by Cross Training Publishing,
1604 S. Harrison Street
Grand Island, NE 68803
1-800-430-8588

DEDICATION

I dedicate this book to the players and coaches I have had the privilege of coaching and coaching with the past twelve years. My greatest desire has been to intensely pursue winning without ever compromising my beliefs, values, and integrity. I am the first to admit that I am not perfect, but I hope that somehow our paths having crossed would have made them think of Jesus a little bit more.

From Arcadia High School, Glendale Community College, Phoenix College, Scottsdale Christian, and now Phoenix Christian High School, I have coached and been a part of teams that had great players and coaches.

I cannot possibly list them all, but I am thankful for the roles they have played in my life. I salute Mike Andrade, Matt Broek, Dean Cerimeli, Scott Comfort, Cameron Conder, Greg Davis, John Duer, Lofton Duer, Jason Evans, Scott Gesicki, Fred Haeger, Ken Hakes, Chuck Hammond, David Hernandez, Garry Howard, Steve Isaac, Tim Kohner, Pat Lavin, Kurt Minko, David Murphy, Aaron Nance, Jim Rattay, Tim Rattay, Glen Ridinger, Steve Rosholt, Tony Sherman, Jeff Smith, David Tefteller, Mark Vander Giessen, and Mark Wardian. I have gone to battle many times with these men, and many others to whom I am indebted.

Probably my most rewarding season was when I was the line coach at Glendale Community College and we went 1-8. We had revival. Kids were coming to Christ every week. It was awesome. I will never forget those days and pray that others will not either. Jesus Christ wants to be the center of our lives.

I believe we are to use our ministry to build men, and not men to build our ministry. My coach at Penn State, Joe Paterno, was once asked which of his teams was his best. His response was, "I guess we will have to wait twenty or thirty years and see what those young men become and do with their lives, and then I'll tell you which was my best team." I hope and pray you all will become everything Christ wants you to be.

SPECIAL THANKS

A special thanks to Lee Brimmer, Sherrana Hampton, Linda Ryland, and Rebecca Oughton for the many hours of typing, reading, and editing of this book. Without your efforts this project would not have been possible.

Also, I want to thank the following people for contributing ideas and materials to this book as well as my chapels: Don Price, Mike Bickle, Steve Isaac, Bud Brown, Tom Wilson, Bob Oughton, Josh McDowell, Dan Scott, and Lester Summerall.

I also want to acknowledge the greatest family in the world; my wife, Yelena, and daughters, Carissa and Blakeley. Yelena, thank you for being my best friend, and girls, I am so proud to be your daddy. I am thankful for a family that loves Jesus.

CONTENTS

PREFACE

This book consists of outlines and sermons that have been presented to the Phoenix Suns and the Arizona Cardinals during the past nine seasons. The topics chosen for this book give way to the title, *Intensity With Integrity*.

Intensity with Integrity. There is nothing worse than people that want to win at all costs. Those who have no morals, ethics or integrity. They will cheat, lie and break any rule to win. Equally as bothersome are those men and women who have integrity, but have lost their zeal, drive, motivation and passion to do and be their very best.

1 Corinthians 9:24-27 says, "Do you not know that in a race all the runners run, but only one gets the prize? Run in such a way as to get the prize. Everyone who competes in the games goes into strict training. They do it to get a crown that will not last; but we do it to get a crown that will last forever. Therefore I do not run like a man running aimlessly; I do not fight like a man beating the air. No, I beat my body and make it my slave so that after I have preached to others, I myself will not be disqualified for the prize." Christians should never be accused of lack of preparation and commitment, causing a loss, and then chalking it up to the "will of God."

Colossians 3:23 says, "Whatever you do, work at it with all your heart, as working for the Lord, not for men,." When we give it all we have, and we do it for God, we are winners, regardless of what the scoreboard indicates.

We need both intensity and integrity. There is a generation of young people that needs parents, coaches, teachers, ministers, and others in authority over them to model the pursuit of goals and dreams while living in the boundaries set out in God's word. We give up and quit too easily when it comes to marriage, school, and life. Some will never become all that God has intended because they have become sidetracked and lost their focus. Others live as though the rules do not apply to them. They may have determination, but will step on anyone and do anything to get where they want to go.

It is my prayer that through reading this book, many will come to know the love of Christ, and others will grow stronger in their relationship with Him. I also pray that as a result of this book, you will have chosen to have "intensity with integrity."

1

MARKS
OF
MATURITY

Positive Under Pressure
Sensitive to Others
Mastered their Mouth
Peacemaker, Not a Troublemaker
Patient and Prayerful

Five Marks of Maturity

Christian maturity is a process determined by our character and attitudes. Spiritual growth and maturity are not based on age, appearance, academic/educational status, or by achievements. Christian maturity begins in the hearts of God's people. One of my favorite quotes is, "You can teach what you know, but you will always reproduce what you are." Knowledge can be taught on philosophies, Biblical knowledge, etc., but we always reproduce what we are. Our children are a perfect example of how our lives are reproduced in terms of character and maturity.

I overheard two businessmen talking. The one businessman said to the other, "I can't believe you ripped me off the way you did! You even claim to be a Christian!" The other businessman replied, "Just because I'm a Christian doesn't have to affect the way I run my business!" Our spiritual walk and maturity should touch every area of our lives whether it be in our family, in our choice of friends, in our church, or in our work place.

There are five marks of Christian maturity, character, and attitude that we can follow. The first one marks our maturity under pressure. Are we POSITIVE UNDER PRESSURE? The Bible tells us in James 1:2 "Consider it pure joy, my brothers, whenever you face trials of many kinds." Our Christian maturity will reflect our joy during difficult times. The testing of our faith produces endurance. It matures us and completes us. We may not like the difficulties we are facing, but we can be thankful for the end result. It is a mature attitude to "count it all joy" during difficult times.

An example I would like to use would be that of Kevin Johnson of the Phoenix Suns. Kevin has endured many difficult trials the past couple of seasons. He has missed quite a few games due to a variety of injuries. This has caused him a difficult couple of years. Yet, to watch him grow under these circumstances has been amazing and encouraging! Sometimes we have to take our hands off someone when we know God is working and dealing in their life. It is a difficult process to watch, knowing the Lord is maturing and completing people and bringing them into what they are supposed to be. Kevin is now in the playoffs and doing quite well. I read in a recent sports column that he has the top field goal percentage for the playoffs and he is second in assists for the playoffs.

It still amazes me how God brings things together in HIS time! What comes out of us when we are "squeezed?" Are we positive under pressure? Some people say that when "the heat is on" is when our character is really formed. I used to believe that also, until I really started to think about it. I came to the conclusion that when "the heat is on" is when our character is *revealed!*

I like this little poem by J. Fred Lawton:

"When the Pressure is On"

How do you act when the pressure is on?
When the chance for victory is almost gone,
When Fortune's star has refused to shine,
When the ball is on your five yard line?

How do you act when the going's rough?
Does your spirit lag when breaks are tough,
or is there in you a flame that glows
brighter as fiercer the battle grows?

How hard, how long will you fight the foe?
That's what the world would like to know!
Cowards can fight when they're out ahead...
The uphill grind knows a thoroughbred!

You wish for success? Then tell me, son—
How do you act when the pressure is on?

As a football coach I have seen this revealed not only in myself, but in other coaches, referees, players, and parents. I believe our character is formed when we are abiding with God. Character is formed when we consider our conduct, our lifestyle, and how we respond to pressure. What is our behavior and attitude? How might we change that according to our Christian maturity? A real mark of a mature Christian is one who is POSITIVE UNDER PRESSURE.

Secondly, a mature Christian is SENSITIVE TO OTHERS. I have noticed this especially in athletes, pastors, coaches, and many others. As you watch people you can tell who are and who are not sensitive to others. Athletes are constantly having people pull at them. You know they must reach a point when all the signing and autographing may become a major nuisance. You can sure tell the ones who have a little more maturity about them. They are the ones who understand the obligation and know that they are setting an example regardless of the nuisance. James 2:8 says, "If you really keep the royal law found in Scripture, 'Love your neighbor as yourself,' you are doing right." There is something special about looking out for our neighbors and being sensitive one to another. There is something special about using a kind word or sending a much needed letter. Sometimes that may be just enough in creating new hope or sharing direction in someone's life. Being sensitive to the needs of others can really make a difference!

Commitments made at an early age may stick through to our adult years. I interviewed David Woods while he was playing for the Golden State Warriors. During the interview he quoted many verses of scripture. There came a point when I asked him about some of the commitments he made early in life. He told me that during a church camp, while he was in the fifth grade, he made a commitment to read the Bible everyday! He stated that in the past 15 years he had only missed three days of his Bible reading commitment! Our sensitivity to others will not only make a difference in our own lives, but in other lives as well.

Thirdly, a mature person has MASTERED THEIR MOUTH. I am still amazed at the number of people I know, whether they are in my office, on the playing field, or at various events, that feel they have a license to just "let it rip," when it comes to the way they talk! A mature person has somehow come to the point in their life where they have shown self-control in regards to the way they speak. Ephesians 4:29 says, "Do not let any unwholesome talk come out of your mouths, but only what is helpful for building others up according to their needs, that it may benefit those who listen." The Bible is firm in stating that no corrupt communication should come from your mouth, not a little, not some, but NO corrupt communication come from your mouth! There are times we try to rationalize and say, "Oh, yeah, but I needed it in this particular instance."

A trait of a mature person, regardless of the circumstances, is the ability to master their mouth. The Bible says in James 1:26, "If anyone considers himself religious and yet does not keep a tight rein on his tongue, he deceives himself and his religion is worthless." Ephesians 5:4 says, "Nor should there be obscenity, foolish talk or coarse joking, which are out of place, but rather thanksgiving." Yet, we as Christians know at many times, that although we know these scriptures, do we always follow them? We must be a DOER of the Word and not just a HEARER of the Word. When we know and see the commandments we need to take inventory of our lives. The Bible says in Matthew 12:34, "...For out of the overflow of the heart the mouth speaks." Therefore, we must take heed to what comes out of our mouth as it is reflective of our heart. A mark of maturity is a mastered mouth. If we have failed previously, now is the time for repentance, of going on with the Lord, and being more Christlike today than we were yesterday.

Fourthly, a mature person is a PEACEMAKER, not a troublemaker. As a coach I have had many opportunities to apply these principles. I was once accused by another coach of recruiting and "stealing" football players from other schools. I was going to respond to his accusations by returning a video I had accidently received and enclosing a note. But, on the same day of my contemplating to write the note I was holding a Bible study for the Arizona Cardinals. The message was on being a peacemaker, not a troublemaker. I prayed about this situation and came to the conclusion that I would mail the video back to the coach without a note. I am happy to say the relationship and situation has been resolved and things are much better.

The point is that we have choices to make in our lives. I guarantee you that most of us, if not all of us, are at odds with someone in our life. The circumstance may have been brought on by ourselves or by someone else, but our choice is to be a peacemaker or a troublemaker. Mature people can make wise decisions in regards to relationships and daily decisions. There is something about the mature person and how they use their wisdom to handle certain situations. The Bible tells us in Ephesians 4:3, "Make every effort to keep the unity of the Spirit through the bond of peace." We need to be reconciled to people. Jesus was even at odds with some people. Remember those who hung Him on the cross? Romans 12:18 says, "If it is possible, as it depends on you, live at peace with everyone." It stresses the importance to us to be peacemakers. Instead of causing more conflict, we need to pray for wisdom and ask God to bring about change in a difficult situation.

Finally, a mature person is PATIENT AND PRAYERFUL. A patient and prayerful person has a faith about tomorrow understanding answers may not have come today, therefore, waiting until tomorrow. A patient person has the understanding that God works all things out in His perfect timing. Hebrews 6:12 says, "We do not want you to become lazy, but to imitate those who through faith and patience inherit what has been promised." We have a tendency to give up too easily these days. We tend to give up on dreams, hopes, or what God is calling us to do. Somehow, because the timing is not what we are expecting, we give up. Circumstances do not always go the way we have planned, but there is a certain maturity in those who are patient and prayerful. These people are resolved to the fact that God has the perfect timing for everything. These people continue to pray and do not give up.

Wileen McKennon once said, "Press on, nothing in the world

can take the place of *Persistence*.. Talent will not; nothing is more common than unsuccessful people with talent. Genius will not; unrewarded genius is almost a proverb. Education will not; the world is full of educated derelicts. *Persistence and determination* alone are omnipotent."

These five steps of maturity give us a chance to reflect on where we stand in our Christian walk and challenge us to seek changes that are necessary in our life. Whether it be mastering our tongue, being a peacemaker instead of a troublemaker, or handling our attitude under pressure, I challenge you to make these changes.

TIME OUT:

1. Where do you stand in your Christian walk? Are you where you should be in your walk with Christ?

2. Pray and ask God for a "clean-up" in your life and wisdom in following His mature steps.

3. Make a commitment today to change your lifestyle and read the Bible everyday.

2

THE GOAL OF OUR INSTRUCTION

Love From a Pure Heart
Clear Conscience
Sincere Faith

THE GOAL OF OUR INSTRUCTION

I believe the keys to moving forward are better leadership and a clearer purpose. I often speak to men and women who lead others and tell them that the key to better leadership is to have clearer goals. We need to know what we are doing, and why we are doing it. There has to be a thought out philosophy for why we exist and what we are doing. The same is true on any athletic team. There has to be a philosophy for the offense and defense you run. The same is true in the preparation for weekly games. There are decisions to be made on how to attack an opponent or what coverage to run on defense. We need a strategy on how we are going to win this game.

We need to teach and admonish with wisdom. It is not enough to teach alone. It must be done with a strategy and with wisdom. We never want to stand before anyone as a leader without a strategy as to what we want to produce. In Colossians 1:9 Paul said he was praying for the church at Colosse to be filled with the knowledge of God's will through spiritual wisdom and understanding. This is one of the characteristics Paul was trying to produce in those he led.

Colossians 3:16 says, "Let the Word of Christ dwell in you richly as you teach and admonish one another with all wisdom, and as you sing psalms, hymns and spiritual songs with gratitude in your hearts to God." Paul also wanted the Word of God to dwell in this church richly. He also wanted to produce gratitude in their hearts toward God. In Colossians 4:5 Paul wrote, "Be wise in the way you act toward outsiders; make the most of every opportunity." Paul was also concerned about how this church treated outsiders or those who were not in Christ.

As a preacher, I must have an idea of what it is I want to communicate in the next four weeks, four months, etc. There must be a planned purpose and goal as well as a philosophy on how I am going to get there. I believe the Bible gives a strategy and wisdom to setting and attaining our goals spiritually. Colossians 1:28-29 says, "We proclaim him, admonishing and teaching everyone with all wisdom, so that we may present everyone perfect in Christ. To this end I labor, struggling with all his energy, which so powerfully works in me."

Much is demanded of those in leadership roles. There is a Day of Judgment and evaluation coming for those in leadership. 1 Corinthians 3:10-15 tells us the Day of Judgment does not have to be an awful or dreaded day. I believe there is a way to conduct yourself in this age where we can say, "Praise God, there is a day of revealing where God will vindicate our efforts that no man even knew about, and also the sacrificial striving after Him, when no man saw what we were doing." I want God to say to me on that day, "You have lived wisely and were productive during your time on earth." I do not want Him to say, "You told the story well, you were a 'good' guy, but you did not produce anything."

God forbid that my life would be summed up that way. In 1 Corinthians 3:10 it says, "By the grace God has given me, I laid a foundation as an expert builder, and someone else is building on it. But each one should be careful how he builds." Are you clear about your present goals? If you are in ministry, do you know what and why you are teaching what you are? I know we do not all have a teaching role, but do we know why we say the things we do to our children? Howard Hendricks said, "If you lack goals, any road will get you there." It is a statement that stands true in athletics. We come across teams that just do not seem to be focused.

The Boston Celtics during their "heyday" were a team that had a strategy. If you do not know what you are trying to produce spiritually in the lives of other people, it will probably be "wood, hay and stubble, and things that will burn on the Day of Judgment." I believe each of us has a calling. Each of us has a place where God wants to use us. Are you clear as to what God is requiring of you?

We are interested in reproducing what God has placed in our hearts for the sake of the Kingdom of God. God's method is instruction. You can instruct through speaking and exhorting others to do various things, and you can instruct through example. Instruction is God's example of bringing about the goals you have in mind. We need to be able to say, "This is what God says." We do not have to be dogmatic in all the minor doctrines of the Word of God, but we do have to be dogmatic in areas such as morality and conduct.

The following topics I want to discuss are three qualities that we, as leaders, should try to encourage in others. It is important to note that we cannot *make* anyone follow us. They *choose* to follow because somehow we have gained their respect. The Bible speaks of these qualities in 1 Timothy 1:3-5 when Paul was warning Timothy of the others who were preaching false doctrines. He wrote, "As I urged you when I went into Macedonia, stay there in Ephesus so that you may command certain men not to teach false doctrines any longer nor to devote themselves to myths and endless genealogies. These promote controversies rather than God's work—which is by faith. The goal of this command is love, which comes from a pure heart and a good conscience and a sincere faith."

Love From a Pure Heart

We want to see the people we lead start loving others. Love comes from a pure heart. Purity, meaning no mixed motives, and not loving for the wrong reasons. There are four aspects of love we want to develop in our people.

1. We want to motivate people toward a *love for God*. We need to ask ourselves, does that person enjoy God? Does he enjoy God as a top priority in his life? We need to ask ourselves, "Do we enjoy the Lord?" There might be some of us that have to admit, "No, I cannot say that I really do enjoy Him." God, to some, is a list of rules and regulations. That is all right. We can change that. There is a tomorrow in God every day. Hallelujah! We need to have communion with God. The worst feeling in the world, as a leader, is to try to preach a message when we have lost our first love and

have no communion with God ourselves. There is never a time when I feel more inadequate than when I stand before people and try to preach His Word, yet have not spent quality time with God myself.

I believe our message and our preaching flows out of our relationship with God. If you enjoy God and His presence, people will see you enjoy Him. It will be evident in your lifestyle as well. If we have to admit right now that we really do not enjoy God, we need to desire and cultivate an attitude to where we do genuinely enjoy His presence. You can never give a seminar on loving God and motivate people to love God, unless you truly love Him yourself. God will reproduce His joy and love through you.

2. We want to develop *love for the body of Christ and for fellow believers*. We are part of the same family. We need to realize when we speak of the Body of Christ, we are all part of that same body. We would not say to our foot that we have no need of you, nor to our eye, or any other part of our body. So it is with the Body of Christ. We each make up part of the body. Ask God for wisdom as to how we can motivate others to walk in love. The Bible says in Ephesians 4:3, "Make every effort to keep the unity of the Spirit through the bond of peace." A priority for loving our brothers and sisters in Christ needs to be developed.

We can only give away what we have. I like the story of the beggar at the gate called Beautiful. He was begging alms of Peter and John. They said, "Silver and gold have I none, but such as I have, I give unto thee. In the Name of Jesus, rise up and walk." They did not have any silver and gold, but what they had they gave.

An intellectual communication is very ineffective. We need to be passionate in our prayers for others so that they will become convinced, and become men walking in love. We cannot give up on others. Understand they are going to blow it from time to time. 2 Corinthians 1:4-6 says we can only minister out of that which we have received. If we are only about receiving intellectually, we will only give away intellectually through doctrines and precepts about God. There is nothing worse than trying to communicate something you have learned from a book rather than a brokenness and yieldedness unto God.

3. God also wants to produce in His people a *love for the lost*. This is called evangelism. In Matthew 9:37-38 Jesus says, "...The harvest is plentiful but the workers are few. Ask the Lord of the harvest, therefore, to send out workers into his harvest field." I like verse 36 which says, "When he saw the crowds, he had compassion on them, because they were harassed and helpless, like sheep without a shepherd." Jesus loved people and He knew He could make a difference in their lives.

We, who have experienced the love of God ourselves, ought to weep and pray for those who do not know God. We need to ask God to give us a burning desire to reach others for Him. I remember when I was attending Penn State University and preaching to fellow students in the middle of the campus, locking the doors and preaching in a dorm room, or a group of us sitting out in the middle of the Quad singing about Jesus. We were not ashamed of the Gospel. Romans 1:16 says, "I am not ashamed of the gospel, because it is the power of God for the salvation of everyone who believes: first for the Jew, then for the Gentile." I have often said there are only two things in life worth living for–to know God more intimately each and every day and to make Him known. Lost humanity is why we are here. Otherwise, Jesus could go ahead and take us home. People that do not know Jesus go to hell.

4. God wants to develop in us a *love for our enemies*. This last aspect of love is a difficult one. Matthew 5:44 says, "But I tell you: Love your enemies and pray for those who persecute you." Loving your enemies does not seem logical. It is impossible without the power of the Holy Spirit working within us. If you will notice, Jesus did not tell us to "put up" with our enemies, but to love them and pray for those who persecute us. I think all of us can admit this is difficult. Nonetheless, I must begin to see these four aspects of love being produced in people that I am leading or I am a failure. It is possible to be successful as a Christian man without being successful as a Christian leader. I believe this will be a standard with

which God will use to evaluate our effectiveness as a leader–the ability to produce these things in others. Maybe not before thousands, but one on one. The reason God tells us to love our enemies is not because it makes us look righteous. God says it makes us more like Him. Because we want to be like Him, we do it.

It is not enough to walk in love. We must walk in love with a pure heart. James 3:16 talks about selfish ambition and bitter jealousy. There are three sources of conflict. The first one would be when two people have a clear cut conviction that they will not compromise on, therefore, the difference of convictions causes conflict. This type of conflict is a valid one. However, most of our conflicts occur because of the other two sources: selfish ambition and bitter jealousy. Selfish ambition means that you want something for yourself. Bitter jealousy can happen when someone else attained what you wanted. Rarely is the conflict because you have set a holy and righteous standard in which you will not be moved.

We need to lay down our selfish ambitions and bitter jealousies and lead people to purity of motive in these areas. These wrong attitudes must be confessed specifically. I believe we need to admit it, take personal responsibility for it, and specifically confess it to be cleansed from it. It does not matter how wrong you are by mistreating me, for if I get offended, I am wrong. Proverbs 17:9 says, "He who covers over an offense promotes love, but whoever repeats the matter separates close friends." Then in Proverbs 19:11 it says, "A man's wisdom gives him patience; it is to his glory to overlook an offense." These scriptures bring to mind the following story.

I heard a message by Mike Bickel years ago and he said that he made a commitment he called "DOC." "DOC" meaning that he would not be Defensive, Offended or Complaining. Whenever God would show him that any of these traits existed in him, he would repent of it immediately as if something evil was in his heart. That day I made the same commitment. I said, "Lord, I do not want to be defensive, offended or complaining." If we do not come forth in purity of heart, then we are not successful as leaders. We really cannot measure our success by any other standard. We cannot choose to just keep the machinery running. We think it is better than nothing to at least have someone there working in that group as a leader. This is not true. By doing so, it may be communicating that it is acceptable to walk with God and live impure.

There is a difference between seeking and attaining. God did not say we had to attain to be qualified to lead. He said we need to SEEK to be qualified. We would never preach on any issue if we had to first attain the qualities we are speaking about. We are still in the "process," and no one has attained them yet. Until we SEEK these qualities, we will never receive the wisdom on the specifics of them. As stated earlier, there is nothing more frustrating than to speak on something you are not pursuing yourself. We will be so general we will not be effective. There is no way to be a minister of the Gospel without living holy before God in our private lives.

God wants to produce love that flows from pure hearts. This is the goal of Christianity. We as leaders need to pursue this in our own prayer closet. A message that is prepared in the mind only reaches the mind, but a message that is prepared in the heart reaches the heart.

TIME OUT:

1. Do you love your enemies? Read Matthew 5:44.

2. Do you have a love for the lost?

Clear Conscience

The subject of a clear conscience tends to be a very delicate area. People are very vulnerable and feel condemned because their consciences are not clearly instructed. We need to be clear on the various issues of the conscience. The only other alternative is bondage. It is frustrating being a leader and discussing different issues that are convicting, because I do not want to see people become confused and fall into bondage. If we exaggerate the truth, it will bring them into bondage. Then, on the other hand, if we underscore certain issues, or understate them, it will not be of help.

There is only one thing that frees man and that is the truth. John 8:32 says, "Then you will know the truth, and the truth will set you free." The difficulty in leadership is getting people to understand and see clearly. It is unresting at times as a leader because I am not always able to see clearly. This brings us back to God, saying, "God, give me the wisdom."

Three Realms of a Clear Conscience

The first area of a clear conscience is to *avoid legalistic service.* Many people witness, fast, pray and read the Bible to win God's favor. Rather, these should be done with a desire to cooperate with God. There is nothing more erroneous than seeking to win the love of God. Romans 5:8 says, "But God demonstrates His own love for us in this: While we were still sinners, Christ died for us." If He loved us when we were His enemy, how much more does He love us now that we are His children?

There needs to be an obedience to the Holy Spirit. God does not speak to us on nine issues all at the same time. The Bible tells us there is a season and a time for everything. He will put His finger on different areas in our lives that He desires us to work on at that time. Be sensitive to the Holy Spirit. When God does pinpoint a specific area in our lives, obey the Holy Spirit. We need to teach people to obey the Holy Spirit when God puts His finger on something specific in our lives. Do not say, "I don't know how to do that." Pursue it yourself and see how God works in your life. When we serve God with legalism, it becomes a trap. We will never enjoy God, not because we do not love Him, but because we will be condemned all the time. People become condemned in their conscience because they are misinstructed. They try to be something God is not asking them to be. 1 Timothy tells us of how some people become "shipwrecked" in their faith. I believe many people who serve God from a legalistic standpoint are vulnerable to being "shipwrecked."

There was a time in my Christian walk when I would feel condemned much of the time. I would try to witness to five people a day. I tried to pray an hour a day, read the Word an hour and half a day, and fast once a week. There comes a time that you catch your breath and you say, "God, this is so hard. I don't even know who You are." He then says back to us, "I'm your Father. I am not a taskmaster." The No. 1 tool the devil uses to try to destroy people is lack of clarity or uncertainty in what God requires of them.

A second area we want to discuss is *legalistic obedience*. This would include gray areas such as drinking wine, the Sabbath, food, movies, makeup, etc. We need to be cautious with gray areas. You may say, "Well, I don't think drinking wine and some of the other topics are gray areas." Keep in mind, it is human nature to gravitate toward tradition and away from the Word of God. I am implying that we should be wise and cautious in areas such as these. Also, remember people are always against what they do not understand.

Many times we have too many unnecessary restraints put on us that the Bible does not oppose. The Bible says in Romans 14 to watch out for the brother who is weak in faith. The brother who is weak in faith is the one who walks in restraints that God did not put on him. Walking with restraints put on by man and not God will kill the joy in your life.

The final area of a clear conscience is the area of *being accepted by faith and not by works*. God is motivated within Himself to love us. We do not have to motivate God to love us. Too many people try to win God's approval. We do need to pray, read the Word, and go to church in cooperation with God as his disciples, but not to get Him to love us more. He already loves us. Ephesians 2:8, 9 says, "For it is by grace you have been saved, through faith–and this not of yourselves, it is the gift of God—not by works, so that no one can boast." People are relating to God on the basis of what they have done or by their good works, rather than what Jesus did on the cross at Calvary. They are trying to obtain what they already have—love and acceptance from God. When they fail and sin, they run away from God. But, those who relate to God on the basis of what Jesus has done, when they fail and sin, they confess it and get right with God. Therefore, you can stand boldly in His presence.

If the enemy can trick people into relating to God on the basis of what they have done for God, he can destroy them with condemnation if they fail. He can also destroy with pride if they succeed. What if a man prays three hours a day? He will be the most arrogant man around if he is relating to God on the basis of what he has done rather than on what Jesus has done. Discipline and legalism are the same outwardly, but the attitude is different. Sometimes we are trying to motivate God to love us, or are deeply concerned about looking good to others. You can have legalistic prayer times where you have committed to God and others that you are going to pray an hour a day. This is legalistic prayer when you make such a commitment based on the importance of how others will view you rather than it being a desire of your heart. If you have to churn it up every morning because of the commitment you made, it can become legalistic. We need to learn to be moved by the leading of the Holy Spirit versus the energy of the flesh. We should teach people to obey their conscience. Do not walk one way when your conscience is telling you something else.

TIME OUT:

1.   Do you ever go against your conscience?

2.   Do you ever try to get God to love you more through your service and obedience?

Sincere Faith

A real, genuine faith is that which will keep you in a place of joy even under pressure. I have found that these three perspectives have blessed me.

First, God is loving and He desires my best. He is looking out for me and He has me in the palm of His hand. He cares for me and has the circumstances of my life under control.

The second perspective about God that helps me is realizing that He is all knowing. He knows what is best for me. I can have a sincere faith that is real and genuine because I know He loves me and He knows what is best for me.

The final perspective is that God is all powerful and He can do nothing but the very best. God has the power to do anything. If He was all loving and all knowing, but was not all powerful I could not have a sincere faith. I would not know if He could come through or not. I can have a faith and a hope because I know these things about my God. Hope is having an eternal perspective while faith is having confidence in present things. Hope leans more toward eternal things. A sincere faith is not false. It is real. It helps you keep life in perspective. It does not look through rose-colored glasses. It can handle problems head on knowing God is with us.

Others know when you are sincere. People know when you are sincere about your faith, love, and trust in God. There is nothing worse than someone who is false and insincere. We need to learn to be real and genuine. If we are going to lead, we need to lead people into love with a pure heart, a good conscience and a sincere faith. We can only measure the success of our ministry by seeing if we are producing these qualities in the lives of those we lead.

TIME OUT:

1. Is there any area that you are not being sincere?

2. Do you have faith that God is all powerful and can do anything? Do you put any limits on God?

3

SPIRITUAL WARFARE

Who is Our Enemy?
Be Prepared For Your Enemy
How to Win the Battle
Why We Need to Win

SPIRITUAL WARFARE

This chapter is dedicated to understanding the battle and spiritual war that we are engaged in. Hosea 4:6 says, "my people are *destroyed* from lack of knowledge." Another translation says, "my people *perish* for lack of knowledge." In this chapter, we will discuss whom we are at war against and what to do about it. We will also discuss why we need to be engaged in this battle and the need to win.

Any athletic team goes into a battle or contest with as much knowledge about their opponent as possible. They need to know their strengths and weaknesses. They want to give themselves as much opportunity to win as possible. If we do not know we have an enemy, and do not understand what he is trying to do to us, the Bible says we will be destroyed or perish. The devil can take advantage of us when we are not aware of his schemes. The Bible also tells us how to win this battle. We have to go in with a game plan against the enemy of our soul. It is one thing to know he exists; it is another to be prepared in our battle against him. We will read through many scriptures, that if applied, will help us gain the knowledge we need to win the battle at hand.

I am not one of those people who sees a demon or devil behind every bush. I am also not one who believes all of our problems are because of the devil. I believe many of our problems are because of a lack of discipline in our lives or a lack of self-control. As I deal with people, I also believe that many people are ignorant of the spiritual world that exists. The spiritual world is more real than the physical world. It was the spiritual world that called everything that exists into being. The spiritual world is real even if we do not see it. We do not see God, angels or demons. We cannot even see the spirits of human beings, and yet, the Bible speaks of all of these things.

Who Is Our Enemy?

Ephesians 6:12 says, "For our struggle is not against flesh and blood, but against the rulers, against the authorities, against the powers of this dark world and against the spiritual forces of evil in the heavenly realms." Our struggle is against anything that opposes God and His Word. Our struggle is not against people (flesh and blood), but our battle is against the spiritual forces behind the wickedness that is so prevalent in our society. Too many times we battle against people until we come to the understanding our REAL battles are the forces behind those people. John 10:10 says, "The thief comes only to steal and kill and destroy; I have come that they may have life, and have it to the full." This is the mission statement of the devil. The devil wants to steal from us, kill us, and would ultimately love to destroy us by sending us to hell.

Hell is the second most talked about subject in the Bible. The Bible says in 1 Peter 5:8, "Be self-controlled and alert. Your enemy the devil prowls about like a roaring lion looking for someone to devour." There is a devil and he is not on our side. He does not want good for us, he wants destruction. He is against us. He opposes us. 2 Corinthians 11:14 says, "And no wonder, for Satan himself masquerades as an angel of light." The devil may try to act like he is on our side, and may sometimes try to say the right things to us. But, even when the devil says a truth, he is setting up a lie. The devil opposes the truth. John 8:44 says, "You belong to your father, the devil, and you want to carry out your father's desire. He was a murderer from the beginning, not holding to the truth, for there is no truth in him. When he lies, he speaks his native language, for he is a liar and the father of lies." Jesus was speaking to the Pharisees when he made these statements. He said there is no truth in the devil. He was telling the Pharisees that if you do not stand for the truth, then you are of your father, the devil.

The chief thing we need to know about the devil is, he opposes the truth and he influences others to oppose the truth. Since he tries to make a lie look like the truth, and the truth look like a lie, we have to be very discerning people to not be deceived by our enemy. That is why he comes as an "angel of light." He often looks good, but we need to understand that he is deceptive. He is a schemer. The Greek word for scheme is "schematose." This means to make the truth look like a lie, and a lie look like the truth. He brings confusion and he is the author of lies.

Jesus asks us to report for battle. He tells us to stand up for the truth and to oppose those people and influences who stand against the truth. We do not have to be argumentative, but we do not have to back down either. When we enlisted in the army of the Lord, we said, "Lord, I am yours. Show me what to do." This battle takes place on a daily basis even if we do not always recognize or see it. There is a battle raging in the humanistic philosophies on our college campuses. The battle rages around the political arena on issues such as abortion. The battle goes further down into the elementary schools where we find literature that teaches "alternative lifestyles," such as homosexuality, to first graders. The battle rages for truth in high schools as people try to keep the Bible off campus, but freely hand out condoms. Yes, we have an enemy and we need to understand who he is and what he is trying to do.

TIME OUT:

1. Memorize 1 Peter 5:8 and John 10:10.

2. Do you recognize who the real enemy is?

Be Prepared for Your Enemy

Ephesians 6:10-11 says, "Finally, be strong in the Lord and in the strength of His mighty power. Put on the full armor of God so that you can take your stand against the devil's schemes." Remember, the devil is a schemer. He will even use the instrument of music to place thoughts in our minds. Remember, the devil was choir director in heaven. Jimmy Hendrix once said, "If you can control the music of the people, you can control the people."

If we will be strong in the Lord and the strength of His might, and put on the full armor of God, we will be able to stand against the enemy. It does not happen through our own strength. It happens through God's strength. It happens by applying the truth of His Word. He gives us the armor to put on. It says in Ephesians 6:13-18, "Therefore put on the full armor of God, so that when the day of evil comes, you may be able to stand your ground, and after you have done everything, to stand. Stand firm then, with the belt of truth buckled around your waist, with the breastplate of righteousness in place, and with your feet fitted with the readiness that comes from the gospel of peace. In addition to all this, take up the shield of faith, with which you can extinguish all the flaming arrows of the evil one. Take the helmet of salvation and the sword of the Spirit, which is the word of God. And pray in the Spirit on all occasions with all kinds of prayers and requests. With this in mind, be alert and always keep on praying for all the saints."

I could use a full chapter to speak about the full armor of God, but I will say in short, it all revolves around the Word of God. Faith comes from the Word of God. The faith in which we take up our shield comes from the Word. Peace comes from a right relationship with Jesus and others. The Word guides us to those peaceful relationships. The gospel is God's Word about salvation. We have to make Jesus Christ the Lord of our life if we are going to engage in this battle. Andre Waters of the Arizona Cardinals, and a few other players in our Bible study speak of how they daily put on the full armor of God. They actually wake up each morning, and spiritually speaking, put on each piece of the armor.

The armor that we are to put on could be compared to that of the football equipment a player would put on when getting ready for a game. The breastplate of righteousness would be like the shoulder pads a football player wears. He also wears a girdle under his uniform, which could be symbolic of our loins girded with truth.

Our feet shod with the preparation of the gospel of peace is like the cleats a football player uses to dig in to get where he needs to go. The shield of faith could be like the arm pads and other pads players wear to raise against the enemy to fend them off and protect themselves from injuries. The helmet of salvation would be like the football helmet which protects the head.

TIME OUT:

1. Make a commitment to read the Word daily for 15 minutes.

2. Put on the "spiritual armor." Read Ephesians 6:10-18.

How to Win the Battle

Ephesians 4:27 says, "and do not give the devil a foothold." If we are going to win this battle, we should never give the devil an opportunity. I was doing the marriage counseling for a former Phoenix Sun and his fiancee when they informed me that they were living together, but not involved sexually. My response to them was twofold: Number one, I don't believe you because I feel by giving the devil an opportunity, he most certainly will take advantage of the opportunity. My second point was that even if you are not sexually involved, you are violating two scriptures. First, the Bible says not to give the devil an opportunity, and you are doing that by living together before marriage. Secondly, the Bible says to avoid even the appearance of evil, and you are not obeying that scripture, because you are most certainly giving the appearance of evil by living together. They are happily married now and are vitally serving the Lord in their lives. We need to make sure we do not allow the devil to take advantage of situations that we give him.

2 Corinthians 2:11 says, "in order that Satan might not outwit us. For we are not unaware of his schemes." Remember the battle is for the truth. The devil will try to convince us that the way in which

we are walking is acceptable. Every step you take away from God's Word and His truth, the devil will pat you on the back. We are to not be ignorant of his schemes. Give him no advantage. When we give the appearance of evil, or when we give the devil an opportunity, we are not walking according to the truth of God's Word. The Bible says in Matthew 10:16, "I am sending you out like sheep among wolves. Therefore be as shrewd as snakes and as innocent as doves." The Bible also says in 1 Corinthians 10:31, "So whether you eat or drink or whatever you do, do it all for the glory of God." An example of this would be that of a mother who does not spank publicly for all to notice. I believe in spanking our children, but in the day we live, people will accuse you of child abuse if you are not careful. We need to be shrewd and innocent.

It is only when we walk according to the truth that we bring glory to God. The Bible says in Ephesians 5:11, "Have nothing to do with the fruitless deeds of darkness, but rather expose them." We should not be walking according to the darkness but we should be exposing the darkness to the light. The Bible also says in 1 Thessalonians 5:21-22, "Test everything. Hold on to the good. Avoid every kind of evil." We are to examine everything carefully. Then, after careful evaluation, if things match up to the truth, we are to hold on to them. If they do not match up to the truth, we are to abstain from them.

That is why I tell people all the time to analyze what I and other preachers have to say. If someone says something contrary to God's Word, then you hold on to God's Word and throw out what others have to say. Too many times we jump in, believing everything everyone tells us. We need to eat the meat and spit out the bones. Most of the time we do not examine everything carefully, nor do we always know if it is backed up by God's Word. This is why it is important to read and study the Word of God so that we are not lead in a false direction. We need to do this if we want to win the battle.

Another key scripture concerning what we are to do to win the battle over our enemy is in James 4:7, which says, "Submit yourselves, then, to God. Resist the devil, and he will flee from you." The first step we have to take is to submit to God. We must take that situation to the Lord and ask Him to help us. THEN, we resist the devil and stand against him and all that he represents. The Bible says, "he will flee from you." If we want to keep the devil on the defensive, we have to keep our lives submitted to God. We need to abide in Christ. John 8:31-32 says, "To the Jews who had believed him, Jesus said, 'If you hold to my teaching, you are really my disciples. Then you will know the truth, and the truth will set you free.'"

The reason people are not free is because they do not know the truth. You cannot know the truth apart from God's Word. People seek for truth in astrology, palm readers, friends, etc. But you will only know the truth through God's Word. Then, once we know the truth, we need to abide in the truth. In other words, stay there! Live it on a daily basis. We cannot forget it or become neglectful of the truth (James 1:25). That is when our lives are truly submitted to God and when we will know the freedom we have in Christ. The devil tries to put us in bondage, but Jesus wants to set us free.

Another key scripture is 2 Corinthians 10:3-5, which says, "For though we live in the world, we do not wage war as the world does. The weapons we fight with are not the weapons of the world. On the contrary, they have divine power to demolish strongholds. We demolish arguments and every pretension that sets itself up against the knowledge of God, and we take captive every thought to make it obedient to Christ." The weapons we have are divinely powerful. The weapons we use are not like weapons used in a physical battle. We do not use guns, tanks, hand grenades, knives, or anything of a physical nature. We do not see the weapons we possess, because it is the Word of God that is our weapon. It is called the Sword of the Spirit. We do not see our shield of faith, but nonetheless, we have it. The shield helps us extinguish all the fiery darts of our adversary.

Verse five also speaks about strongholds and imaginations. Many of us get bound up by alcohol, fear, sexual thoughts, and different obstacles that become strongholds in our lives. Others are plagued by imaginations. An imagination is something that does not really exist. I believe the devil intrudes and tries to bring stress into our lives by making us think people are angry with us when they are not. He uses our imagination to create doubt, fear, and lies. Again, that is why it is important for us to remember to "take every thought captive to the obedience of Christ" (2 Corinthians 10:5). That is the key ingredient in winning the battle against your enemy. When we have a thought, and we are not sure where it is coming from, take it to God. Ask Him to help you obey the truth. Do not dwell on the thought, but give it to God. Go to Him in prayer. Ask Him for help in obeying the truth and following through.

TIME OUT:

1.   Choose a couple of these scriptures to memorize. James 1:25; John 8:31-32; 2 Corinthians 10:5.

2.   Do you give the devil any opportunities?

3.   Are you giving the appearance of evil in any area?

Why We Need To Win

1 John 3:8 says, "He who does what is sinful is of the devil, because the devil has been sinning from the beginning. The reason the Son of God appeared was to destroy the devil's work." God wants to destroy the work of the devil, and He is going to use you to do it. Many people are obeying a lie instead of the truth. God wants to use us to reveal His truth. Jesus wants to set people free. Luke 10:19-20 says, "I have given you authority to trample on snakes and scorpions and to overcome all the power of the enemy; nothing will harm you. However, do not rejoice that the spirits submit to you, but rejoice that your names are written in heaven."

God desires for our names to be recorded in heaven. Names are recorded in heaven when we get saved and make Jesus the Lord of our life. God wants to use us in this process. The Lord said in Mark 16:15, "..Go into all the world and preach the good news to all creation." The Bible says there is no other name given among men whereby we must be saved. Why do we need to understand the battle, fight the battle, and win the battle? It is because there are souls and lives at stake. Lives are being destroyed by the devil, and we, who have God's truth, need to take it to them.

Jesus said in John 10:10, "..I have come that they may have life, and have it to the full." An abundant life is God's desire for everyone. There are many Christians who do not enjoy an abundant life. The only reason we do not have an abundant life is because, we are not armed with the truth of God. Somewhere in our lives we are believing a lie if we are not experiencing the abundant life.

You can have an abundant life even in the midst of very trying circumstances because abundant life is something that takes place on the inside of us. It is not dependent upon circumstances. 1 John 4:4 says, "You, dear children, are from God and have overcome them, because the one who is in you is greater than the one who is in the world." What is happening on the inside of us is much more important than what is happening on the outside. There are so many people in the world who have never experienced this abundant life. They have great loads and heavy burdens. Jesus said in Matthew 11:28-30, "Come to me, all you who are weary and burdened, and I will give you rest. Take my yoke upon you and learn from me, for I am gentle and humble in heart, and you will find rest for your souls. For my yoke is easy and my burden is light." We need to lead people to the Savior and we need to teach them the truth of God's Word. The devil wants to keep people from experiencing God's abundant life. The Son of God wants to destroy the works of the devil. We need to recognize who our enemy is, and what to do about him. We also need to understand the reason why God wants us to do these things. He wants us to do these things so we can experience victory in our lives, and help others experience it as well.

We need to put on our armor to be prepared for battle against the enemy, the devil. He is the god of this world. The Bible says in 1 John 2:15-17, "Do not love the world or anything in the world. If anyone loves the world, the love of the Father is not in him. For everything in the world—the cravings of sinful man, the lust of his eyes and the boasting of what he has and does—comes not from the Father but from the world. The world and its desires pass away, but the man who does the will of God lives forever."

KINGDOM OF THE WORLD

Satan - the god of this world
(2 Cor. 4:4)

KINGDOM OF GOD

JESUS IS LORD
(Philippians 2:11)

World Principles:

1. Seeing is believing.
2. Wise.
3. Save your life.
4. First.
5. Great.
6. Ruler.
7. Exalted.
8. Front seat.
9. Look to your own interests.

10. Receive much.
11. Make your good deeds known.

12. Love is a feeling and is conditional.

13. Love grows cold.
14. Hate your enemies.
15. Retaliate.
16. Judge.

Bible Principles:

Believing is seeing. (John 20:29)
Fool. (1 Cor. 3:18)
Lose your life. (Matt. 16:25)
Last. (Mark 9:35)
Least. (Mark 10:43)
Servant. (Mark 10:44)
Humble yourself. (Luke 14:11)
Back seat. (Luke 14:10)
Look to the interest of others. (Philip. 2:3)
Give much. (Luke 6:38)
Keep your good deeds secret. (Matt. 6:3)
Love is a commitment and is unconditional. (John 13:34)
Love never fails. (1 Cor. 13:8)
Love your enemies. (Matt. 5:44)
Forgive. (Col. 3:13)
Judge not. (Matt. 7:1)

17. Cover mistakes. — Confess mistakes. (Prov. 28:13)

18. Human might and human power. — Not by might, nor by power, but by my Spirit. (Zech. 4:6)

19. Eat, drink, be merry–tomorrow we die. — Man shall not live by bread alone. (Matt. 4:4)

20. Drown your sorrows. — Be filled with the Spirit. (Ephes.5:18)

21. It is possible. — All things are possible to him that believes. (Mark 9:23)

22. Check your stars. — Search the scriptures. (John 5:39)

23. The scripture was written by man. — All scripture is inspired by God. (2 Tim. 3:16)

24. The Bible is outdated. — All Heaven and earth will pass away, but My words will never pass away. (Matt. 24:35)

25. Jesus was a good man. — Jesus is Lord. (Philip. 2:11)

26. Jesus is dead. — Jesus Christ is the same yesterday, today, and forever. (Hebrews 13:8)

27. Jesus is not coming again. — I will come again and will take you to myself. (John 14:3)

28. I'll never worship Jesus Christ. — Every knee shall bow and every tongue confess that Jesus Christ is Lord. (Romans 14:11)

4

ATTITUDES THAT WILL WIN THE WORLD TO CHRIST

Compassion
Creative
Sacrifice
Cooperation
Commitment

Compassion

The attitudes displayed by the four men that carried the paralytic to Christ were "whatever it takes" attitudes (Mark 2). If somehow we could tap into these attitudes, we could affect our world to a greater degree.

The primary thing that we need in terms of soul-winning and winning our world to Christ, is the compassion these men had. They somehow, someway, wanted to get their friend to Jesus. When you think about the alternatives of where people go when they die, there are really only two. Do we have compassion to look upon our world and the people we come in contact with, helping them realize that those two options are available to them? What are we going to do about it? The Bible says in Matthew 9:37-38, "Then he said to his disciples, 'The harvest is plentiful, but the workers are few. Ask the Lord of the harvest, therefore, to send out workers into his harvest field.'" The passage goes on to tell of the compassion God had on them because they were like sheep without a shepherd. When you think about a picture of our society today, I believe our society is like a sheep without a shepherd. Where do we, as Christians, fit into the great scope of God's plan of winning this world to Christ? It really does happen one by one. It happens first and foremost, because we care. Spiritual work is done by spiritual people whose hearts God has filled with compassion.

If you read through the book of Acts, they were filled with boldness. Oh, that we could be filled with the same kind of boldness they had! These men realized that they were not going to get their friend to Jesus unless they made the effort. They knew that by getting their friend to Jesus, their friend would leave differently from the way he came. So it is with people that meet Jesus today.

Their lives are never the same. The world is not going to be won to Christ accidentally. It will be won by people purposing in their heart to do something about our society. These men decided that they loved their paralytic friend, and their compassion motivated them to do something to change his situation.

The first thing that God has to do in our hearts is cut us to the quick, and give us a compassion for our world. There are times I have to remind myself that Acts 1:8 says, "But you will receive power when the Holy Spirit comes on you; and you will be my witnesses both in Jerusalem, and in all Judea and Samaria, and to the ends of the earth." Where was Jesus standing when He said that? He was standing in Jerusalem. Sometimes we get our eyes on the utter-most parts of the earth, but forget our own Jerusalem. The influence we should have begins in our neighborhoods, our homes, and places of employment. I believe God has a purpose for us being in that particular neighborhood or at that particular job. We are not there by accident.

The only things that are significant in life are the things that are done in light of eternity. Money only has significance when you use it in light of eternity. Your time only has significance in light of eternity. How can you lay up your treasures in heaven except by giving of your time and your money? It is easier to give a check than it is to give of your time. This world is not going to be won to Christ by accident. We have to make it the purpose of our hearts. God has to somehow touch them and show them that they need to be concerned about the people around about them. Is God bringing anyone to your mind that you need to be concerned about, or have compassion for? What about their eternal destiny? Where are they going to go when they die?

In 1 Corinthians 3, Paul speaks of how one person sows, another waters, and God gives the increase or the harvest. If some do not sow and some do not water, God can never harvest the seed. We need to plant and water seeds on a daily basis. People are won into the kingdom because someone is concerned enough to sow a seed, then someone else comes along and waters it, and eventually God does the harvesting. We cannot change someone's will, but God can. God's Spirit eventually ushers them into the kingdom. We need to understand that we need to be planting and watering on a daily basis. We need to have compassion as these men had, the compassion to get their friend to Jesus. Remember, people do not care how much you know, until they first know how much you care.

TIME OUT:

1. Read Matthew 9:37-38 and 1 Corinthians chapter 3.

2. Do you have compassion for those who do not know Christ? Pray and ask God for a deeper concern and love for those around you.

Creative

Secondly, these men were creative. How many church services have you been to where they cut a hole in the roof and lowered a sick person down in front? It was so crowded they could not get through the door. They very easily could have said, "Well, we'll come back tomorrow, or maybe we can get Jesus' attention on His way out." There are so many excuses that they could have used, but their compassion was so strong that they would not sell out. They would not be denied.

We need to know our society if we are going to reach them. We, as Christians, need to be creative in reaching this world. I believe everyone has something that they can do. The Bible says in 2 Corinthians 3:6, "He has made us competent as ministers of the new covenant–not of the letter of the Spirit; for the letter kills, but the Spirit gives life." The point is, we are all ministers of the new covenant. We are all about the ministry of Jesus Christ. God has gifted different people in different ways. Therefore, we should use and be creative with the gifts God has blessed us with.

Sacrifice

Thirdly, these men were sacrificial. Being sacrificial is surrendering to Christ to a greater degree. When people start to step out and relate to Jesus Christ, and begin to identify with Him publicly, that is when they start to be effective in winning their world to Christ. We need to identify with the Lord. There is something that is important for us to understand about the story of Jonah, and also about our own lives. Why did Jonah not want to go and preach to the Ninevites? He did not like them. He did not want to go and preach to them. He wanted God to destroy them. How can you reach someone if you have anything against them? The book of Jonah 1:17 says, "But the Lord provided a great fish to swallow Jonah, and Jonah was inside the fish for three days and three nights." Notice the scripture says "provided." In other words, I do not believe you can argue that this is the will of God. Chapter 4:6 says, "Then the Lord God provided a vine and made it grow up over Jonah to give shade for his head to ease his discomfort, and Jonah was very happy about the vine." In the very next verse it says God provided a worm. It attacked the plant and it withered.

I think that many times, in terms of being sacrificial, we are bathing in our luxuries too much, which distracts us from our purpose. Sometimes, God has to send a worm to knock the props out from under us. He wants us to get back to work and be about God's business. Just like God appointed the fish and the plant, God also appointed the worm. That discredits the health and wealth gospel that teaches you are supposed to be healthy, wealthy and wise and nothing is ever supposed to be wrong. At times, when God wants us to do something, He has to knock the props out to show us what is more important. Too many times, we get so caught up in doing other things that distract us from what is really most important. God calls us to make a sacrifice.

TIME OUT:

1. Has God given you any creative ideas?

2. What sacrifice are you willing to make to lead your friends to Jesus?

Cooperation

While preaching in a certain city, I asked someone how the churches in that city got along. The response I received was, "Fine, we haven't killed any of them and they haven't killed any of us." There is a real problem in the body of Christ in terms of cooperation. Everyone seems to be protecting and more concerned about their own "turf."

When it comes to unity, some people differ in their definition. Some people want to build a wall between themselves and others and call that unity. Another concept of unity is "the big fish, little fish unity." It is okay if you are the big fish swallowing the little fish, but what about the little fish? Is that really unity?

Cooperation is incredibly important when it comes to the kingdom of God. There is a saying that I have written in the back of my Bible and quote many times to some of the teams I work with, "It's amazing how much can be done when no one cares who gets the credit." It happens to athletic teams all the time. People start bickering because someone wants the credit.

In God's eyes, the one who planted and watered will be recognized one day. He may not even know that the seeds he planted were harvested. One day, because he planted those seeds and was faithful in the planting and watering, God is going to recognize him. He will see those people in heaven. He may have never known those he gave a tract to or shared Christ with, who came to know the Lord.

In Mark, chapter 2, there was great cooperation needed by these men. Cooperation to cut a hole in the roof, place the man on a pallet, and using four ropes, to start lowering him down. They had to get him to Jesus. Just think if one of them had decided that they wanted to be a little stronger than the other, or a little quicker than the other, what would happen to the paralytic? He would end up in worse shape than when he started. The point is, these men went to such an effort to bring the paralytic to Jesus. Without cooperation from them all, it would not have worked.

The same type of cooperation is involved in bringing someone to Christ. Prayer is part of the cooperative effort in bringing someone to Christ. Not only is prayer part of the cooperative effort, but it is the backbone of any ministry. When someone tells me that they have been praying for me, it thrills my heart. When people begin to pray, it is because of cooperation. The Bible says in Hebrews 3:13, "But encourage one another daily, as long as it is called Today, so that none of you may be hardened by sin's deceitfulness." Think of cooperation this way: one of four men had to come up with the idea of hoisting the paralytic up on the roof in the first place. The others had to yield to another's idea as being a better idea than their own. The point is, we have to cooperate if we are going to win our world to Christ.

TIME OUT:

1. In what ways could you be more cooperative?

2. Write down different ways that churches, organizations and people can cooperate more with one another.

Commitment

The quality of commitment is very evident in the four men that carried the paralytic to Jesus. They were committed to get their friend to Jesus.

John Wesley was also a man who demonstrated commitment. He traveled 250,000 miles in 40 years, preached 40,000 sermons, produced 400 books, and knew ten languages. At 83 he was annoyed that he could not write more than 15 hours a day without hurting his eyes and at 86 was ashamed that he could not preach more than twice a day. He complained in his diary that there was an increasing tendency to lie in bed until 5:30 a.m.

These men in Mark chapter 2, were willing to do whatever it

took in completing their mission. No obstacle was too great. There was nothing that they were not willing to do. They had already missed out on the best seats for the service. They had given up comfort to carry a man several miles. Their backs and legs were probably aching. There was no price too much to pay. The only thing they could see was their goal, to get their friend to Jesus so He could change his life from his present state.

Athletic teams that are committed are the ones that usually end up on top. Talent can sometimes let you down. Teams that keep their eye on the goal and the dream do not care what price has to be paid. It is worth whatever effort to see the dream fulfilled.

Running wind sprints, lifting weights and practicing are worth it because they have a dream. These men had a dream. They wanted to see their friend healed. They were committed to see that dream fulfilled.

These quotes sum up what commitment really means. "Those who can remain...are a rare breed." I don't necessarily mean win, I just mean remain. Hang in there. Finish. "Stick to it until it is done." But unfortunately, very few of us do that. Our human tendency is to quit too soon. Our human tendency is to stop before we cross the finish line. Jesus said, "Remain in me, and I will remain in you."

Vince Lombardi said, "I firmly believe that any man's finest hour is that moment when he has worked his heart out in a good cause and lies exhausted on the field of battle, victorious."

What kind of commitment do you have in bringing people to Jesus? Are you willing to be called in the middle of the night to help a friend? Do you view your money and material possessions as something to be used for the Kingdom of God? People are usually committed until it costs them something: time, money, or effort! Remember, people don't care how much you know until they know how much you care. Are you committed?

TIME OUT:

1. How committed are you? Does your commitment start to waiver if it costs you time or money?

5

RELATIONSHIPS

The Counterfeit of Love
Friends
What to Look for In A Wife
Marriage
For Husbands
How to be a Great Dad

The Counterfeit of Love

Love is the desire to *give* at the expense of oneself. However, lust is the desire to get at the expense of others and God. Many young people mistake lust for love. So many children growing up never see love displayed in their homes, therefore, it only makes sense that they know very little about it.

When hormones start to flow, and a member of the opposite sex is giving a person the attention they so desperately need, it is hard to decipher lust from love. Many relationships that could have developed into something stronger and better, are sometimes destroyed by the lust that runs rampant and unchecked. In other words, the relationship was never really given the needed time to determine if there was true love at all, because lust was in the way. When all that is desired in a relationship is to "find some space and make out," you can be sure that the majority of that relationship is lustful, with very little, if any, love. The desire of at least one of the parties in a lustful relationship is to get and not to give. How sad it is to be bound to a relationship where all the other person wants is some form of sexual gratification. My suggestion to those caught in relationships such as this, is to run quickly and get out of it. However, if you are married to someone like that, the commitment has already been made, so now you need to work on the relationship and not run from it!

Test your relationships!! Find out what the basis for them really is. Do not be fooled by the smooth talk of someone who tells you they love you, but in reality all they care about is self-gratification. Josh McDowell, a friend and Christian author says that sex is about one fourteenth of a marital relationship. What are you going to do with the other thirteen fourteenths of your time, if you marry based on lust and not love? You will probably argue and seldom enjoy one another's company.

Lust does not care about others, but only taking care of self. It also has no regard for God either. It says, "I want what I want, when I want it."

Love is the desire to give at the sacrifice of self. I would rather take care of the one I love and be concerned about how they feel than to fulfill my own wants and desires. Love is willing to wait!

TIME OUT:

1.   Remember that the devil is the master of counterfeit. Do not let him tell you that lust and love are one in the same. Lust is the cheap imitation of love. It is not even close to what God tells us love is. It is not the real thing.

2.   Read what real love is in 1 Corinthians 13.

Friends

The key to any relationship is friendship. The ability to enjoy one another's company and doing things together is what it takes to make a marriage work. My wife, Yelena, is my best friend. I used to get intimidated at the thought of being friends. I thought that was just a cop-out. I thought it was just a way to say, "I really do not want to hang around you in any romantic sense." I have continually learned the value of being friends in marriage. It enhances the romantic times because of the shear joy of wanting to be together.

To be able to laugh together, cry together and share your deepest thought is to really trust and care. Many marriages are on the rocks today because the couple never learned to be friends. Oh, yes, they love one another, but they never have learned to enter into one another's world and enjoy their company.

My wife and I are very different in many respects, but that does not keep us from enjoying the differences. We have our little spats here and there, but we have learned to appreciate those differences and believe God has brought us together to complete one another. In other words, I appreciate my wife's eye for detail, because I am more of a "just the facts" person. I appreciate my wife's enjoyment of being a homemaker, because I tend to get involved in too many activities away from home.

If you think about one of your closest friends in your life and why you are such close friends, it probably would include things like you trust one another, you like many of the same things, and have personalities that complement one another. Now why is that so different from men's and women's relationships? Most marriages that I know are ones where opposites definitely attracted, and yet there is a great complementing of personalities. Trust is something that only comes with time. Enjoying many of the same things is also something that comes with time and experiencing many things we never dared to do before. My wife really enjoys football and basketball games these days, and I can get a kick out of going shopping (for a couple of hours anyway). The only way it came about was by trying what the other person likes. I think that is called being friends.

TIME OUT:

1. Who is your closest friend in life? Why?

2. In dating and marriage make friendship a priority. Remember that a friend doubles the joy in life and halves the sorrows.

What to Look for in a Wife

In March of 1990, the Phoenix Suns Basketball Team was young, and many of them unmarried. Therefore, I felt it important to share from God's Word on what to look for in a wife. They certainly could have their choice of women, so, it was very important to know what qualities to look for in a mate. Many women have the wrong motives in regards to money, popularity and sex.

Here are some of the qualities we discussed found in Proverbs 31:10-31.

Her husband has full confidence in her. Verse 11 discusses the importance of having trust and confidence in the one you choose. If you cannot trust her, do not choose her!

She does him good and not harm. This is especially true with those in the public eye. It is important that she be a person that others speak well of; that she have a good reputation, and not one that is sleazy or slothful. She can bring good by developing a good name, being a good mom and wife, and by praying for her husband and supporting him in every way.

She works with eager hands. Verse 15 says she gets up while it is still dark and verse 17 says she works vigorously. Verse 18 actually says her lamp does not go out. I think this shows the hard work it takes to be a good wife and mother. As the little saying goes, "A mother's work is never done."

Entrepreneurial spirit, she uses her mind. I believe in the mom that stays at home whenever possible. Yet, the Proverbs 31 woman maintained a creative mind while at home. Verse 16 says, "She considers a field and buys it; out of her earnings she plants a vineyard." We need to support this creative side of women whether at home or not.

A Servant. This is why a lot of women seem to have a real closeness with God, because they learn to serve their families. Jesus said, "The greatest among you shall be the servant of all." It is impossible to be an effective wife and mother without a servant's heart. I told the players to find someone who has this kind of spirit.

Clothed with strength and dignity. Strength is an inner quality. Dignity is to be worthy, honored and esteemed. We can see what a person physically wears, and so it is with a woman's strength and dignity. Her inner qualities can be seen by others just as well.

When she speaks, wisdom comes from her lips. The greatest quality a person can attain is that of wisdom. It is a sister to discretion. Women who lack wisdom are obvious. Find a woman who knows how to handle herself when she speaks, when in public, or how she contains herself in a negative situation. She will instruct the children in the ways of God.

Good Manager. Whether a domestic engineer or in the corporate field, she knows how to run her household. With all the cleaning, cooking, ironing, washing, and other responsibilities of a home, can you expect this woman to be a good manager?

Her husband has a good name because of her. Verse 23 says that a woman with great character brings respect to the husband because of her good name. Awesome! I believe my wife does this for me. Because of the way she conducts herself, I have a better name.

She fears the Lord. Obviously the woman you choose needs to be a Christian. Otherwise, the Bible calls that being "unequally yoked" in 2 Corinthians 6:14. You need to find a woman who wants to honor God with her life and loves Him with all her heart. Without a commitment to God, people can break their vows in a heartbeat. She needs to be more committed to God than she is to her husband. Her commitment to God will keep her from the ways of the wayward wife. 1 Peter 3:4 tells us that the real beauty of a woman is that of a gentle and quiet spirit. The emphasis is on the inner beauty as being more important. Proverbs 31:28 says, "Her children arise and call her blessed; her husband also, and he praises her." They recognize her hard work and commitment over the years.

Charm is deceptive, beauty is vain. Find the woman that fears God, for it does not matter how pretty your mate is. Do not be taken in by just the beauty, or just the charm, find out whether she fears the Lord or not. There are many attractive women out there. If they do not fear God, forget them, they might break your heart. Proverbs 1:7 says, "The fear of the Lord is the beginning of knowledge, but fools despise wisdom and discipline." If they lack wisdom or the fear of the Lord, find someone else!

TIME OUT:

1. Write down on a piece of paper what you are looking for in a mate. Are they similar to the characteristics discussed?

2.   If you are married, pray to be all God wants you to be in your marriage covenant. If you are unmarried, pray for God to bring the right person. Pray that you as well, will have these Godly characteristics.

Marriage

I have heard it said by Dr. Edwin Louis Cole that, "Marriage is the closest thing to heaven or hell that you will ever experience on the face of the earth." I believe this is very accurate in most cases. There is usually not much room for the "in between stuff" in marriage. It is either great or bad. I am very thankful that I have one of those marriages that is a heavenly one. With the divorce rate still well over 50 percent, there are many marriages experiencing a "hell on earth."

I am glad that my wife and I have taken time to get to know one another. We have gone to seminars, read books, and done other projects that relate to being a good husband and wife. I came from a home with a mother, father, and three boys. Like most men, I had very little understanding of women. The biggest area that we lack training in, is being a husband or a wife. Anything else in life needs training before you can get a license. Not with marriage! We are thrown out there and expected figure it out. I encourage you to read some good books on marriage. Go to at least one seminar or couple's retreat every year or get involved in the marriage class at your church.

It has been said that there are two great motivators in life: the desire for gain, and the fear of loss. I hope that both can motivate us to nurture our marriage relationship. We should be motivated to gain a better understanding of one another. We risk the possibility of losing the relationship if we do not pay close attention to it.

I recently read a survey on marriages that was very upsetting. It indicated that 75 percent of women felt their marriages were in trouble, while only 25 percent of men felt that their marriage had problems. In other words, 50 percent of the men surveyed, whose marriages were in trouble, did not even realize it. Hebrews 13:4 says, "Marriage should be honored by all, and the marriage bed kept pure, for God will judge the adulterer and all the sexually immoral."

My biggest prayer these days is for young people to understand that God has ordained marriage, that it is good. He desires that it be for a lifetime and a heavenly experience.

TIME OUT:

1.   Regardless of how many years you have been married, go to a marriage seminar or get away once a year. If you are not married, read some books and educate yourself as much as possible.

2.   Read Hebrews chapter 13 and Ephesians chapter 5.

3.   What kind of marriage do you desire to have?

For Husbands

Have you ever thought about the concept that God is not answering your prayers if you do not live with your wife in mutual respect, honor and love? That is exactly what 1 Peter 3:7 says, "Husbands, in the same way be considerate as you live with your wives, and treat them with respect as the weaker partner and as heirs with you of the gracious gift of life, so that nothing will hinder your prayers."

Living in understanding with our wives is a command of Scripture. God says to do it. I often get irritated at men who dominate their wives and allow them very little participation in decisions or matters such as finances. Many members of the older generation have a view of the woman being simply the helpmate. Their wives have no active role in decision making. They exist solely to cook, clean, and to take care of the kids. The Bible actually calls the woman the completer of the man. In other words, the man is not complete without her. Many times my wife's "woman's intuition" has saved me from wrong decisions—decisions that could have cost us a large amount of money. Making her a partner in the relationship, and involving her in decision making will please her and solve many problems as well.

To understand our wives, there must be communication. This is where I, and many other men, often fail. Women are more relational by nature and want to be a part of their husband's life by communicating with him. Men tend to be more logical, goal-oriented and conquer-oriented by nature. I heard the example of a couple who were building a house. She wanted a patio in the back yard because that is where relationships are nurtured. All he wanted to know is what it would cost since he is more logical. The key to a healthy marriage is understanding that God has created us differently for a reason. We are complete when we tap into the resource of one another's personality and strengths.

The Bible calls the woman the "weaker vessel." Now, I know a lot of "women's libbers" do not agree with scripture on that point, but it is never-the-less true. Physically and emotionally, God has designed the man to carry the burden in most cases. Men have been called to guide, guard, and govern their homes. This means protecting your wife from harm as well as the stresses of today's society. God tells us we are to respect them as the weaker vessel.

Scripture also tells us that we are heirs together of the grace of life. We were designed to travel this pilgrimage called "life," together. We are not to be two people living in the same home, yet living separate lives, but together! That means we do things together, make decisions together, eat together, and laugh and cry together.

I know we have all heard the teachings of women submitting to the man, but I know very few women who would not respond naturally to a man who loves her, listens to her, respects her opinion, and wants to be a team together in life.

TIME OUT:

1.   Memorize 1 Peter 3:7.

2.   Remember the woman is designed as the weaker vessel. Make sure to take some of the weight off her.

3.   Dwell together in understanding with your wife. Do not strive to change one another, let the Lord do that.

How to Be a Great Dad

There is probably not a greater responsibility in all of life, than that of being a father. It can also be a very rewarding role when we take it seriously. I remember hearing the story of a young man and his father who both kept journals. They had gone on a fishing trip together but had not caught anything that day. In the dad's journal, he wrote that it was a wasted day because they had not caught any fish. But in the son's journal, he wrote that it was the greatest day of his life. He and his dad had spent time together going fishing. As dads, many times we do not realize the impact we are having just by spending time with our kids. I believe a father's role is most important in what our children will become. We need to develop memories that last a lifetime. I remember the time my Dad took me fishing on the Potomac River, and I remember the time he dropped me off at Penn State University, and told me not to allow these Pittsburgh and Philadelphians to turn me into an Eagles or Steelers fan, because we had been Redskins fans our whole lives. It is amazing what a child will remember when it comes to a father's leadership and time. Even small incidents, that may seem irrelevant, can have a big impact on a child in a way we may not be aware.

With Christian Athlete Ministries, we hold a Father/Son, Father/Daughter Basketball Camp that has had a great impact on relationships between dads and their children. I shared these nine points at the Father/Son, Father/Daughter Basketball Camp this past year on, "How to Be an Effective Dad."

1. *Spiritual leader.* A dad has to be a spiritual leader. God has called him to this. He needs to know his children will follow in his footsteps. He needs to know that more is "caught" than taught in life, and when children see their dad reading his Bible, praying with his family, and going to church, they will "catch" that because of the example he sets. They will follow in our footsteps in terms of what we say and what we do. We need to remember "We will reproduce what we are." Joshua said in Joshua 24:15, "..But as for me and my household, we will serve the Lord." As our kids see us trusting the Lord, they will follow. The Bible says if you train a child in the way that he should go, when he is older he will not depart from it. I ask the dads reading this chapter, "Do you pray with your family? Do you take them to church? Do you open the Word of God on a consistent basis?"

2. *Dads need a vision and direction for their families.* The Bible says without a vision, the people perish. Without a father's vision, the family will disintegrate. A man needs to spend time with God and get direction for his family. Ephesians 3:20 says, "Now to Him who is able to do immeasurably more than all we ask or imagine..." We might get concerned about stepping out and doing different things, but God will supply the power and ability to do the things He asks and requires of us. We need to ask ourselves sometimes, "How will I be remembered by my children?"

3. *A dad needs to be a man of integrity.* We earn the right to lead, by doing what we say we are going to do. We have influence–either negative or positive. If we want our influence to be positive, we need to walk in integrity and honesty. When we promise something to our children, we need to come through on our promise. Children do not know the difference between a broken promise and a lie. Do not make promises to your children flippantly. Many times we either say "maybe" or "we'll see." We should try to only say "yes" to things we know we will do. In Ecclesiastes the Bible asks whether we vowed a vow. If you do

make a promise, make sure you come through on it. This is why the greatest example a dad can set for his children is to love their mother. He vowed a vow at the altar to love their mother. When children see us being people of integrity, they will learn to be people of integrity. When they see us coming through on our vows and promises, they will do the same.

4. *An effective dad is a decision maker.* A leader has to be decisive. We have to determine what is best for the entire family. We need to learn to do this in the context of wise counsel, our wife, and even listening to our children. It is important to have a weekly family meeting to go over schedules and talk about what others are feeling. I have found that a weekly family meeting helps to keep life in perspective, and helps the each family member know that his or her opinion counts. Some men have even declined promotions if they thought it was best for the entire family.

5. *A great dad communicates clearly.* We need to learn to communicate what is in our heart, and also listen to what is in our children's hearts. Most parents are more negative than positive, but we need to take our kids on a walk or a drive to find out what they are thinking. That involves listening and talking. I want to communicate to my family that they are the most important people in my life, that I am proud of them, I trust them, I want to listen to them, I am always on their side, and that they can always count on me. They need to know that I pray for them daily. I also want them to know I am flexible and not everything has to go my way. Thomas Jefferson once said, "When it comes to principle, stand like a rock, but when it comes to taste, swim with the current." Great fathers know when to be tough and when to be tender.

6. *Be responsible.* There is no way to be a leader without being responsible. There is a price to be paid. There are both privileges and responsibilities to being a leader. There is a lot of hard work, and tears to be shed. We have to be responsible, both for our actions and our attitudes. We have to be careful about what we set before our children's ears and eyes. I do not want my kids to learn their values from "Rosanne," "Married With Children" or "The

Simpsons." I need to remember that I am responsible for what is being set before them.

7. *Be cooperative.* When the family wants to do something, he is willing to go along. Leaders get cooperation when they are cooperative. Sometimes we have to say "no," but at the same time, cooperation can achieve results.

8. *Be a servant.* Do you expect special treatment, or do you give special treatment? Jesus said the greatest among you shall be the servant of all. In other words, a leader needs to serve. We need to serve our wives and serve our children.

9. *Lead in Love.* The saddest funerals are the ones where the family does not care because they never felt their dad's love. I have never heard an older person say, "I wish I had spent more time at the office." How will you be remembered by your family? People will do anything for someone they know loves them. Love is spelled T - I - M - E. You can buy gifts, and that's nice, but love is spending quality time with your children.

TIME OUT:

1. Are you the spiritual leader of your family? Do you lead by your examples of praying, reading the Bible, and attending church?

2. Have a weekly meeting with your family to talk about your schedule, vacation, and how things are going.

3. Do you spend quality time with your family? Ask them.

7

FIVE WORDS

Situations
Emotions
Thoughts
Beliefs
Actions

Situations

We all find ourselves in a variety of situations. Situations are often uncontrollable. Some we cause by our own decisions and others come upon us virtually unexpected. Situations are places we find ourselves in regardless of how they happen.

A few examples of bringing negative situations upon ourselves are speeding in our automobile and getting in an accident or receiving a speeding ticket. I know of a young man who had to get married and find a job very quickly because he got his girlfriend pregnant. This is a situation that could have been avoided. He brought it upon himself. Using drugs has many negative possibilities also. There is the possibility of death, disease, or addiction. This also can be avoided.

There are situations that people are surprised by, and really could not avoid. They are basically at the mercy of the decisions of others, or the will of God. I used to think that AIDS was only a homosexual disease until I heard of a ten year-old pastor's boy who contracted the AIDS virus through a blood transfusion. This young boy was a hemophiliac, meaning his blood would not clot. So, he received blood transfusions quite often. The blood testing for HIV did not begin until 1985, and many of his transfusions were given previous to that year. When tested, he was HIV positive. This is not a situation he brought upon himself. It was not his decision to be a hemophiliac, or to receive the blood transfusion that gave him the AIDS virus. Still, this is a situation he and his parents are left to deal with. This is one of those unexplainable situations.

The same is true of the family whose 16 year-old son drowned. He was caught in an undercurrent while tubing down the Salt River in Arizona. This was a freak accident. The family did not bring this situation upon themselves, yet they also are left to deal with this tragedy.

If you were born into an alcoholic family, you had no control over that situation. You were born into it. A mate who walks out on you, an athlete who wants to fight, when all you are doing is playing the game, or the business partner who rips you off financially, are all situations you may have to deal with.

One last example of situations that would not be considered under the law of sowing and reaping would be the abuse of children. When children are abused, molested, or violated in any way, they end up having to deal with the scars of that situation for the rest of their lives. They have to decide how they are going to respond. We will discuss the correct way, versus the incorrect way, to respond to the situations we find ourselves in.

We face some situations on a minute-by-minute basis. We are faced with how to respond to another person in conversation, what to do to better relationships, and how to achieve success in various areas of our lives. There is a choice to be made in regards to how we will react. We cannot ignore problems thinking they will go away. Our response is the key to what our action and attitude will be. We either respond based on our thoughts and emotions, or by our beliefs. How we respond will determine the outcome.

The disciples asked Jesus about a particular situation which arose in their day. In John chapter 9, they asked Him who sinned, the blind man or his parents that he was born blind? Jesus responded it was neither this man nor his parents, but it was done that the works of God should be revealed in him. In the future, we will see that it is best to deal with these negative situations based on our belief system in the Word of God, rather than our own thoughts and emotions.

TIME OUT:

1.   Read the story found in John 9:1-12 about the man who was born blind. Think of the various situations in your life, the ones you have caused and the ones you did not bring upon yourself.

Emotions

Dealing with situations in our lives by our emotions will prove to almost always have the wrong corresponding action. Emotions of anger, hatred, bitterness, passion, lust, jealousy and envy, lead us to an action we will not be proud of. Emotions are the things we feel, and a reflection of what is happening on the inside. This is not to say that emotions are necessarily negative. How refreshing it is to see the joy and excitement an athlete shows when he wins a championship, or the thrill of parents at the birth of a child. Emotions can be a wonderful and joyous feeling, but we cannot rely on them to deal with certain situations we face in life.

For example, if I respond to a situation of losing a loved one with the emotions of rage, bitterness or hate, I may well find myself angry at God or saying something I wish I had not. Dennis Byrd broke his neck while playing for the New York Jets during a game in 1992. He could have found himself angered at God if he dealt with the situation from an emotional standpoint. Instead, he dealt with it according to his belief system based on God and His Word. He realized God can use this situation for His glory. If I respond with hatred to a business partner who takes advantage of me financially, or rage toward another athlete because of a gesture or comment, I could very well cuss, kill, fight or do any number of emotional things. The story of Nancy Kerrigan comes to mind. The ones emotionally tied to Tonya Harding tried to take Nancy Kerrigan out of the competition by bringing harm to her. Emotions have to be kept in check. They must be filtered through the truth of God's Word in order to bring a balance to our lives. Do not trust your emotions. They will lead to the wrong action.

Many people deal with their sexual desires on the emotional level rather than filtering them through God's belief system. In turn, they pay a dear price. The result can be emotional heartache, AIDS, other diseases, or an unwanted pregnancy. Tim Kimmell once said, "Never sacrifice the permanent on the altar of the immediate." If we are going to abide by that principle, we need to live life by our belief system based on the Bible, and not our own emotions.

TIME OUT:

1.   What emotions do you struggle with the most? Anger? Lust? Jealousy?

2.   How will you choose to control them in the future? Find scriptures that deal with these areas.

3.   Study God's Word and pray for direction and victory in these areas.

Our Thoughts

As discussed in "Situations," we have different methods of response to our situations. One of them is to respond by thoughts or intellect. Isaiah 55:8 says, "'For my thoughts are not your thoughts, neither are your ways my ways,' declares the Lord." Proverbs 3:5 says, "...lean not on your own understanding." We may not always be able to figure things out.

Our thoughts can be greatly misguided. The devil can influence our thinking by planting seeds in our thoughts or through temptation. The world and the peer pressure around us can do the same. Even my own fleshly, selfish desires can affect what I am thinking, therefore, in opposition to Christ. That is why my thoughts are not a safe way to respond to my situations.

I had a man come into my office who told me God had brought a new person into his life. He was planning on divorcing his wife and marrying this new person. This is absurd. Our own selfish desires combined by the seeds planted by the devil, can try to convince us of anything. Then sometimes we try to spiritualize it by saying that God had placed this new person in our life. The Bible says that God hates divorce. It says we are to stay committed to the vows we made before Him. This is a great example of why we need to not listen to our thoughts. Do you see how perverted one's thinking can get if we do not cling to our belief system found in the Word of God? In 2 Corinthians 10:5-6 it tells us we are to take every thought captive to the obedience of Christ. Take your thoughts and run them through God's Word first.

The only thoughts I can trust are the ones that line up with God's Word. They teach me how to respond to situations that surround me. I pray God brings us to the point where we do not trust our own thoughts, but only His Word. My thoughts, the world's thoughts and thoughts prompted by the devil result in heartache if we act upon them. John 10:10 says, "The thief comes to steal and kill and destroy;...." Jesus said he came to give us life and to give it more abundantly.

Some people have become so perverted that they have thoughts of jumping off of a building or planning other ways of suicide. The two pastors' families previously mentioned, if following their own thoughts, could have found themselves angry with God or blamed themselves for these situations. We have to take those thoughts captive and compare them with God's Word. Responding to these tragedies through our belief system in God brings about a whole new perspective. The Bible says your word have I hid in my heart that I might not sin against thee. The only way to be sure our thoughts are correct, is if they are in accordance with the Word of God. It takes desire and discipline to become familiar with God's Word.

TIME OUT:

1.   Read Matthew 4:1-11.

2.   Memorize Psalm 119:9-11.

3.   Make sure you do not trust your thoughts unless they are based on God's Word.

My Beliefs

To produce the right response to the situations we confront daily, we must respond according to our belief system. This means we must first have a belief system. Everyone has a belief system. The absolute value of beliefs I have is found in the Bible. It is unchanging and relevant to all of life. It should be our guide to dealing with situations that come on a daily basis. In other words, it should be a belief system in accordance with the Word of God.

Rather than dealing emotionally or with our thoughts, we should make it our goal to filter situations through the principles found in the Word of God. Then we will keep our emotions and thoughts in check and deal with life in the way it should be.

The Bible says in Ephesians 4:26, "In your anger do not sin..." Apparently there is a point to anger that has not yet led to sin. Dealing with injustices in our world should make us angry at times, but it should not lead us to bring about more injustice. Abortion is wrong, but so is killing people over the issue. Racism and prejudice in our society is real, but no more than Jesus experienced. We ought to look at how Jesus dealt with racism and injustice against Him. He said, "Father, forgive them for they know not what they do." He taught the people the way it was to be. Matthew 5:44 says love your enemies. Pray for those who despitefully use you and persecute you. This is the way we should deal with the problems we face. Filter them through our belief system before our thoughts and emotions step in.

Romans 12:17-19 says, "Do not repay anyone evil for evil. Be careful to do what is right in the eyes of everybody. If it is possible, as far as it depends on you, live at peace with everyone. Do not take revenge, my friends, but leave room for God's wrath, for it is written: 'It is mine to avenge; I will repay,' says the Lord." We do not need to deal with every situation ourselves, for we know God will bring about penalty in due time without us intervening. We should focus on having pure thoughts like it says in Philippians 4:8. Part of my belief system is as follows:

I believe we should keep our conversation wholesome.
Ephesians 4:29

I believe we should not commit fornication.
1 Thessalonians 4:3.

I believe we should forgive. Matthew 18.

I believe we should stay away from drugs and other things that
harm our bodies. 1 Corinthians 6:19-20.

I believe we should be generous people. 2 Corinthians 9:6.

I believe abortion is wrong. Psalm 139.

I believe in capital punishment. Genesis 9:6.

I believe all these things because I believe the Word of God. We
need a belief system. 2 Timothy 3:16-17 says, "All scripture is God-
breathed and is useful for teaching, rebuking, correcting and
training in righteousness, so that the man of God may be
thoroughly equipped for every good work."

If we believe and trust wholly in the Word of God, we must
then submit the situations which occur in our lives to the principles
found in God's Word. In doing so, we have the assurance that our
actions and responses are in accordance with God. Make it a point
to rely on your belief system first, before your emotions or your
personal thoughts lead to the wrong actions.

TIME OUT:

1. Read 1 Corinthians 6:19-20 and Philippians 4:8.

2. Read Psalm 139 and Genesis 9:6.

3. Determine what your belief system is! Is the Word of God your
absolute final authority? I challenge you to become familiar with
what God says, and not others.

Actions

We all have different ways we respond to situations in our lives. We can respond according to our thoughts, emotions or by our belief system. Our actions will be determined by how we choose to respond. To respond emotionally will produce the wrong action the majority of the time. In a relationship situation, by responding with our thoughts, we will produce the wrong actions. Imagine responding to your thoughts when losing your son in the river or finding out your son has AIDS due to a blood transfusion. Your thoughts would produce bitterness and questioning of God. By responding according to my belief system I understand God is sovereign, God is in control, and there is NOTHING that is going to come to me that is not first filtered through God's love. To respond according to my beliefs rather than my thoughts, will make a great difference in my actions.

If a young person becomes involved with a member of the opposite sex, and does not filter their actions through their belief system, they might emotionally do something they will regret later. The heat of the moment and the passion of the moment may cause them to give in sexually, and cause their actions to be less than they had hoped for. But, if we filter our situations through our belief system, it will cause us to do the right thing. We are all forced to act according to the situations we face.

Life demands a response of some kind. You can watch the battle on a football field or the battle on a basketball court. As you watch the referees' calls notice the reaction of an opponent by possibly throwing an elbow, shrieking a comment or just emotionally flying off the handle. It is evident that we do not always stop to first think of our action. It is easy to tell when someone does not stop to think first about their actions. They usually think after the fact. For those who think about their situation and their response, is it your thoughts or God's thoughts that you are going to respond with? The only way to be sure our actions will be correct is when they line up with the Word of God.

I have heard it said before that we judge others by their actions and ourselves by our intentions. Actions are the barometer of the character of a person. Coach Chuck Knox of the Los Angeles Rams said, "What you do speaks so well I don't have to hear what you say." You will be judged by your actions. The way we produce the right action is to respond with our belief system. Regardless of the situation that comes our way in life, it must be filtered through the Word of God and then we can be sure our actions will be those we can be proud of. Actions eventually produce a lifestyle of habits.

Responding emotionally will produce embarrassing actions. Trying to reason in our own mind rather than the mind of Christ is a dangerous situation. I do not trust my thoughts. I only trust His thoughts. James 2:17 says, "In the same way, faith by itself, if it is not accompanied by action, is dead." Our works have to do with our actions. People will notice our responses to our situations. I was once told by one of my best friends at Penn State, Todd Blackledge, of how he watched me during my times of injury to specifically see what it was I had in my life. My life in Christ impressed him enough that he wanted to investigate the truth of it. People are watching to see how we respond to the situations in our lives, and they will notice if our actions are worthy of respect.

TIME OUT:

1. Do you respond emotionally or with your own thoughts? Do you use your belief system to respond to situations in your life?

2. Do not depend on your emotions or thoughts. Choose to live according to your belief system, which is based on the Word of God.

3. What changes do you need to make today after reading this chapter?

7

GOD'S STRATEGY FOR SUCCESS

Be Clear In Your Direction
Be Confident In Your Desires
Be Committed to Your Decision
Be Corrected By Your Defeats
Be Conscious of God's Dependability

GOD'S STRATEGY FOR SUCCESS

In Joshua 1:7-9, God gave Joshua a five point strategy for success. It says, "Be strong and very courageous. Be careful to obey all the law my servant Moses gave you; do not turn from it to the right or to the left, that you may be successful wherever you go. Do not let this Book of the Law depart from your mouth; meditate on it day and night, so that you may be careful to do everything written in it. Then you will be prosperous and successful. Have I not commanded you? Be strong and courageous. Do not be terrified; do not be discouraged, for the Lord your God will be with you wherever you go."

God never asks us to do anything without His help. God promises to be with us wherever we go. Several years ago, I asked a trick question in the Suns' chapel. I asked, "Would God ever ask us to do something we could not do?" The answer is "yes." He calls us to do things we cannot do all the time. It may be to forgive and pray for our enemies, or to rejoice in the midst of problems. He promises to always be with us and will even work a miracle when He asks us to step out in faith. God always comes through. He did with Peter on the water, as He did with Joshua and the walls of Jericho. He came through for Abraham and Sarah, having their child at old age, and once again He was there for David in his war against Goliath. He will be there for you. It is a promise from God. He tells us to be strong and courageous in the things we attempt to do in this life, whether it be a ball game, a job, writing a book, or in our family life. God has a strategy for us.

Be Clear In Your Direction

God told Joshua the what, the when, the where and the why in Joshua 1:7-9. It is important for us to understand that what you desire to do and what you do well, is usually what God wants you to do. If we are going to have success in the things we attempt to do in this life, we must be clear-minded and we must get our direction from God. This only comes as we spend time with God. God cannot give us direction if we do not spend any time with Him. Usually, the direction God gives us has to do with placing desires in our heart. Psalm 37:4 says, "Delight yourself in the Lord and He will give you the desires of your heart." Some people feel that God is going to give them whatever they want. I believe it means that God will place the passions and desires to do certain things in our heart. When we seek God, and spend time with Him, He is going to give us passion and desire for different things. He is going to make us WANT to do various things. He will even give us the desire to do the impossible–things some people have never attempted before. It is called stepping out in faith. When it comes from God, and we are clear in our direction, we want to attempt it anyway. Proverbs 16:9 says, "In his heart a man plans his course, but the Lord determines his steps."

God not only gives us the desire to do certain things, He usually leads us to do things we do well. It is called His "giftings." God gives abilities, gifts and talents. He wants us to use those gifts and talents for Him and His glory. If someone likes music, many times God will use that gift to glorify His Name. If someone has the talent to play basketball or football, God will use them as well. If someone is creative or artistic, God will use those talents. Sometimes God will ask us to lay those things down, and tell us to go a different direction, but normally He will use the desires and talents we have in terms of leading us.

When it comes to being clear in our direction, we need not shy away from problems. If we are clear in our direction, it does not matter what problems stand in the way. God will see us through those problems. Even the Promised Land had problems. There were seven enemies that had to be defeated in the Promised Land. Even though Moses and Joshua were clear in their direction about the Promised Land, they still had to defeat their enemies. When God gives us a direction, problems just become opportunities to see God more.

I know I was clear in my direction from God when I was 17 years old. I got saved when I was 16 years old, at Suitland Baptist Church in Suitland, Maryland. About a year later, I felt God had called me into the ministry. I remember that as clearly and vividly as though it were yesterday. Many times since then, people have tried to get me involved in insurance and other business adventures where I would make more money. I have been able to decline, because they would take me away from what God has called me to do. That is why we need our directions to be clear and set, so that we stay on course when others pull us in different directions. If we are going to have success in life, we have to be clear in our direction. Our marching orders should come from the Throne Room of God.

TIME OUT:

1. Are you clear in what God is calling you to do in your life? Have you sought the Lord for clear direction? Pray and ask God to reveal His will and calling to you.

Be Confident In Your Desires

After we get our direction, many times doubt begins to come in. There comes a second guessing. We need to remember that the devil always tries to steal the seed that was sown in our hearts. The devil tries to stop things from the beginning. He tried to stop the Christ child from the beginning by having Herod kill all babies under the age of two. He tries to stop our dreams and goals at the very beginning by bringing doubt and confusion.

There are three things that can destroy our confidence. First, past experiences can destroy your confidence. Something negative from the past can be a hindrance in believing God can do something greater in the future. Philippians 3:13 says, "..Forgetting what is behind and straining toward what is ahead..." We need to press toward the mark for the prize of the high calling of God in Christ Jesus.

One of the most difficult obstacles a coach has to do when taking over losing programs is to change the attitude about winning. Losing is a habit, just like winning is a habit. I know when I took over the football program at Phoenix Christian High School, I used to hear the players say, "We stink. We are terrible." People used to talk about how poor the football program was because they had not had a winning season in many years. In the past four seasons we have won four League Championships, a State Championship, and have had a 40-5 record. I do not say that to brag, but to illustrate that you can do what you put your mind to, have a clear direction, and be confident in what you want. Past experiences of losing have to be changed and overcome.

Past negative relationships can become a hindrance to future relationships. Some young women never trust men because of some past negative experience. They might desire a great marriage in the future, but if a man has robbed them in the past, they have trouble trusting men in the future. We have to be confident in our knowledge that God's will for us is to have a happy, healthy and secure home life.

A second area that can destroy our confidence is our emotions. Decisions based on mood can rob our confidence. We need to base our confidence in God's Word and not let our emotions rob us of the truth. That is why it is important not to make major decisions while you are up or down emotionally. Our mind can play games on us when we are tired. You might say, "I don't feel like it." It does not matter how we feel, we need to rest in God and the truth of His Word. God's Word does not change, but our feelings do.

The third area that can destroy our confidence is excuses. If God has placed a desire in us to do something, and given us direction, we need to lay all excuses aside, understanding that He will provide. Excuses such as "I don't have the money, or the education, or the right family," are not valid. Winners always make adjustments, not excuses. What is it God wants you to do? Quit making excuses and go after it with all your heart. Some people never become what God intends for them to be because they make excuses all of their lives.

TIME OUT:

1.   Read Psalm 37:4.

2.   Read and memorize Psalm 127:1-2.

3.   Are you letting any areas from your past rob you of confidence for your future?

4.   Are you making any excuses in your life that keep you from being all you can be?

Be Committed To Your Decision

After God has given us the direction to do something, we need to stay committed to what He has called us to do. We need to stay committed during tough times. The old saying goes, "Tough times don't last, but tough people do." Most people quit just before they experience a break through. Many times we quit because of discouragement.

There are three sources of discouragement I want to discuss. People are the biggest source of discouragement. We worry about what people will think if we fail. We worry about being misunderstood, criticized or ridiculed. Who cares what other people think? We need to be more concerned about what God thinks! Galatians 1:10 says, "Am I now trying to win the approval of men, or of God? Or am I trying to please men? If I were still trying to please men, I would not be a servant of Christ."

Do not let others discourage you. You can be committed to your decision because it is what God has called you to do. That is why we have to be clear in our direction. I have heard it said, that some people understand all of the time, and all of the people understand some of the time, but all of the people will never understand all of the time.

Pressures also become a discouragement. We start feeling stress and we think this is too much responsibility. For instance, there are pressures in starting your own business, and having to trust God for the resources. Maybe others find it in juggling schoolwork with athletics, or responsibilities of raising a family. There are many different reasons we can become discouraged. We need to remember it states twice in the portion of Scripture we read, "Be strong and courageous. Do not tremble or be dismayed, for the Lord your God is with you wherever you go." If we stay committed, God will see us through.

The final source of discouragement is problems. Everyone has problems of various kinds. Everyone seems to want to take the easy road. There will be problems associated with any great work of God. We must not let problems discourage us and cause our commitment to waiver. We need to be like the one who said, "I'm not going over, I'm not going under, I'm going through." When I decide to follow Jesus, I'm going to follow him to the end. I know there are going to be a lot of things that will come up along life's journey, but my goal and desire is to stay committed to the very end.

TIME OUT:

1. Are you committed to your life's purpose? Is there anything that can make you waiver in your commitment?

2. Are you willing to be obedient to God regardless of what He tells you?

Be Corrected By Your Defeats

We need to understand that failure is not final or fatal. The game is not over until it's over. My high school football coach, John Merrick, used to say, "When you fall down, you need to pick yourself up, dust yourself off, and start all over again." We need to quit cursing the darkness and light a candle. People who are successful have failed many times. They have learned from their past mistakes.

Here are a few quotes from basketball coach Dale Brown. "Never be afraid to fail. You will only hold yourself back in the long run." "The role of great leaders is not to try to make athletes look up to them, but rather to get the players to believe more in themselves." "The ability to handle adversity and cope with setbacks is the other key trait successful leaders possess."

There is another quote I read from *Skills For Adolescence* that I found interesting. It reads as follows, "He failed in business in 1831, defeated for Legislature in 1832, he had a second business failure in 1833 and his sweetheart died in 1835, suffered a nervous breakdown in 1836, defeated for Congress in 1848, and then his son died in 1850. Defeated for Senate in 1855, defeated for Vice President of the United States in 1856, defeated once again for Senate in 1858. He was elected President of the United States of America in 1860. His name, Abraham Lincoln."

Many CEO's of FORTUNE 500 companies have failed in business in the past. Once, someone asked me how to get experience. I answered, "By making wrong decisions." Sometimes we make the wrong decision and we get the experience we need not to make that mistake again. We need to be corrected by our defeats.

In Joshua 7:1-13, the children of Israel were defeated by Ai because they had stolen and deceived. They had taken things not their own and put them as their own. They were struck down by the Amorites. As Joshua sought the Lord on this whole issue, God told them they needed to repent and consecrate themselves to the

Lord because they could not stand before their enemies until they had removed the things that were not their own from their midst. Then they would be able to go out and defeat their enemies.

Because they listened to the Lord and were corrected by their defeats, they saw success. First they had to repent for their wrong doing. If we are going to be successful in life, and if we are going to follow through with God's plan for our life, we need to be corrected by our defeats.

TIME OUT:

1. Think of some of the defeats you have faced in your life. What were they and what action did you take?

2. Read Joshua 7:1-13.

Be Conscious of God's Dependability

God promises four things if we obey Him. In Joshua 1:5, He promised *His power.* He said, "No one will be able to stand up against you all the days of your life. As I was with Moses, so I will be with you; I will never leave you nor forsake you." God's power is unlimited. He can do ANYTHING. When we are conscious of our dependency on God, and understand He is dependable, we can do whatever He tells us to do.

In verse five, God promises *His protection.* He said, "As I was with Moses, I will be with you." God shielded Moses with a certain hedge of protection. He gave them a pillar of cloud by day and a pillar of fire by night. He protected Moses for those 40 years in the wilderness and He said He would be with us in the same fashion.

The next promise is a promise of *His prosperity.* Joshua 1:8 says, "Do not let this Book of the Law depart from your mouth; meditate on it day and night, so that you may be careful to do everything written in it. Then you will be prosperous and successful." We have to be careful to do according to all that is written for us to obey. Then He will make our way prosperous, and then we will have success. There is always an "if, then" statement with God. If we obey, then God promises some things. We get it in reverse. We think God's love is conditional and His promises unconditional. That is not true. God's love is unconditional, but His promises are conditional. He says He will only do these things if we first walk in obedience unto Him.

Finally, He promises *His presence.* In Joshua 1:9 it says, "Have I not commanded you? Be strong and courageous. Do not be terrified; do not be discouraged, for the Lord your God will be with you wherever you go." There is not a place in this entire world that we can flee from the presence of God. He says He will be with us wherever we go. There is not a country we can go to where He will not go with us; there is not a back alley where He will not follow, nor is there a ministry situation where He will not be with us. Matthew 10:19-20 says, "But when they arrest you, do not worry about what to say or how to say it. At that time you will be given what to say, for it will not be you speaking, but the Spirit of your Father speaking through you." That is the presence of God. He will be with us in any and every situation.

We need to be conscious of God's dependability. We can do what He has called us to do because He does it through us. We can never do anything on our own. Philippians 4:13 says, "I can do everything through him who gives me strength." But John 15:5 says, "I am the vine; you are the branches. If a man remains in me and I in him, he will bear much fruit; apart from me you can do nothing."

TIME OUT:

1.   Are you conscious of God's power, protection and presence in your life? Write down and discuss some of these areas with a mate or friend. Memorize some scriptures that remind you of these things.

2.   Read Joshua 1:5-9 and memorize Proverbs 16:9.

8

HOW TO BE POSITIVE UNDER PRESSURE

Four Facts About Problems
The Purpose of Problems
How to Handle Your Problems

HOW TO BE POSITIVE UNDER PRESSURE

The book of James is a book about maturity and growth as a Christian. It teaches us about life and how we mature to become more of the person Christ wants us to be. It speaks in realistic terms. It does not sugar coat things and make the Christian life seem to be a rose garden. It shows us how to mature, but at the same time, informs us that it will not be easy. It also states that much of the growth will occur because of the trials in our life.

James 1:2-6 says, "Consider it pure joy, my brothers, whenever you face trials of many kinds, because you know that the testing of your faith develops perseverance. Perseverance must finish its work so that you may be mature and complete, not lacking anything. If any of you lacks wisdom, he should ask God, who gives generously to all without finding fault, and it will be given to him. But when he asks, he must believe and not doubt, because he who doubts is like a wave of the sea, blown and tossed by the wind." In understanding the book of James and how we are to handle our problems, we can learn to be positive under pressure. Even though problems occur, we can still have a sweet spirit and a positive outlook.

Four Facts About Problems

The first fact we need to know concerning problems is that they are *inevitable*. In James 1:2, it does not say *"if* you face trials" but, *"when* you face trials." The emphasis here is on the "when." It will happen. It is not a matter of "if." In life there will be problems. It is simply a matter of "when" they are going to come. Problems are inevitable and they are a part of God's maturing process. You will never get so spiritual that you will never have problems. I believe we can avoid some problems by obeying God's Word. But there are some problems that come regardless of whether we are being obedient to the Lord or not. Problems are inevitable.

The second fact concerning problems is that they are

unpredictable. James 1:2 says, "..whenever you face trials..." We could avoid problems if we knew they were coming in advance. We only face trials when we are not prepared for something. That is how it is with a lot of problems in life. If we had known they were coming, we would have cut them off at the pass. If we knew we were going to be in a car accident, we would not even have gone out that day. If we had known our child would fall and get hurt on those roller skates, we would not have bought them in the first place. Problems are unpredictable.

The third fact concerning problems is that they are *variable.* In James 1:2 it says, "When you encounter trials of *many* kinds..." Many makes sure that we understand that it might not just be one problem. The Greek word for "many" means multi-colored. If you go to the paint store, you will find 42 shades of brown and six shades of chocolate brown. The trials and problems we face in life will come in many different forms and will be different for each individual. What might be a problem for one, may not be a problem at all for another person. By understanding that our trials and problems are variable, it will remind us to bear one another's burdens when we see others facing trials of many different kinds.

The last fact concerning problems that we need to understand is, trials are *purposeful.* James 1:3 says, "because you know that the testing of your faith develops perseverance." That is why the Bible tells us to count it all joy when we encounter trials of many kinds because they have come to produce something good in us. The problems we face have a purpose. God did not allow them to happen to harass us, bring us stress, or even to see how we would handle them. He allowed them to happen to make us stronger in Him. The problems come for a purpose and that is to produce the character of Jesus Christ in a greater way in us. When we get squeezed, we find out how we are going to react under pressure. When things do not go our way, we are forced to make certain decisions. If we do not handle the situation correctly, we will have to take the test again.

My father-in-law has a little saying, "If you don't pass the test the first time, you have to take the test again." My daughter, Carissa, is in the fourth grade. Every Thursday she has a spelling test that I help her study for. If she receives a score of 100 percent she does not have to take the test again Friday. As we get alone with God and analyze our response to problems, we make decisions about how we will react the next time something similar occurs. That is where the trial actually starts fulfilling the purpose, because it starts producing in us what Christ wants in our life. We start becoming positive under pressure when we begin correcting some of our past mistakes.

TIME OUT:

1.   What problems are you presently facing? What is your attitude toward them?

2.   Are you having to take some tests over and over?

The Purpose of Problems

We need to realize that problems have a purpose in our life. God does not allow stress and hassles for no reason. The first reason that God allows problems in our life, is to *purify our faith.* James 1:3 says, "because you know that the testing of your faith..." Our faith needs to be tested. The word "testing" refers to purifying gold and silver. It describes what a blacksmith does when he scrapes the dross or impurities off of silver and gold. The fire heats it up, the impurities come to the top, and the blacksmith scrapes off the impurities. That is what God does in our life. He allows our situations to get heated up, and problems to surface so our faith will be tested. Psalm 119:75 says, "I know, O Lord, that your laws are righteous and in faithfulness you have afflicted me." The Psalmist says we are afflicted by God's faithfulness, and the reason he has afflicted us is to purify our faith. He has a purpose in mind, and that purpose is to make us more like Jesus Christ. He will take us through times of affliction that will test our faith and show us what kind of a person we are.

The second purpose of problems is to *fortify our patience.* James 1:3 says, "because you know that the testing of your faith develops perseverance." We, as Christians, need to know something about endurance and commitment. Christians ought to exemplify perseverance more than anyone else. We need to learn something about routine and being planted somewhere. Too many people change churches and mates at their every whim. That is why, if you ever find the perfect church, don't go there or you will ruin it. Because, there is no such thing as the "perfect church" or the "perfect mate." We all need to learn something about patience. Because no church or mate is perfect, we need to learn to get along. That takes place through patience. Isn't it amazing how God allows irritating people in your life as you are praying for patience? If we want to learn patience, God has to allow the circumstances needed to teach us patience. Usually that is done by bringing people or situations into our paths that try our patience.

God also allows problems in our lives to *sanctify our character.* James 1:4 says, "...that you may be mature and complete, not lacking anything." God wants to bring us to a place of completeness and maturity, where we are lacking nothing. That is a process that will continue until we die or Jesus returns. The trials we face make us more like Jesus when we yield to the Holy Spirit and to what it is God is trying to accomplish through these problems. If God is trying to teach us about love, He usually brings unlovable people into our life. If He is trying to teach us something about joy, He might bring tragedy. To teach us about peace and patience, you may experience a broken dishwasher, kids yelling, a ringing phone and diapers that need to be changed; possibly all at the same time.

God wants to set us apart from the world. He wants to sanctify us and make us different. It would be nice if there were some short cuts, but there are not. In order to produce the faith, patience and character God wants us to have, He uses problems to mold these qualities into our life.

TIME OUT:

1. Write down some of the purposes of your trials.

2. Read Psalm 119:75 and James 1:3.

How To Handle Your Problems

Rejoice! If we want to learn how to handle our problems, we need to, "Rejoice in the Lord always. I will say it again: Rejoice!" (Philippians 4:4). It does not say to rejoice sometimes. It says to *rejoice* always. It also says count it all joy when you face various trials. That is almost masochistic. There really is not any logic. It only becomes logical if we understand what God is trying to do through these trials. When we understand that He is in control and He has a purpose in mind, then the logic takes hold. In 1 Thessalonians 5:18 it says, "give thanks in all circumstances, for this is God's will for you in Christ Jesus." It does not say *"For* everything give thanks." It says, "In everything give thanks." We certainly are not thankful *for* everything, but we can be rejoicing people, even in the middle of our problems. As a matter of fact, I believe what separates us from the non-Christians is our ability to have joy and peace even in the midst of some very trying circumstances.

One man wrote, "I am convinced that life is 10 percent of what happens to me and 90 percent how I react to it." Rather than reacting to everything we need to learn to act. We need to be in charge of our emotions and our thoughts. We should not always react to what someone else says or does. We are in charge of our attitudes. That is why we can count it all joy when we fall into various trials.

A second ingredient to handling our problems is prayer. It says in James 1:5, "If any of you lacks wisdom, he should ask God..." We need to seek God and ask Him why and what to do. Wisdom is seeing life from God's point of view. We need to go to God and ask why this is happening and what should I do about it? What wisdom do you have for me in the middle of this situation? A preacher once said, "Every year you will go through at least one major obstacle." That obstacle can be a stepping stone or a stumbling block. It can be a stepping stone to something greater, or it can cause you to stumble and go backwards. We need to trust God and ask Him for wisdom. The Bible says God will give His wisdom liberally to us if we only ask. We must seek Him in prayer and find out what way He would have us to go.

The final ingredient in handling our problems is to learn to relax. It says in James 1:6, "let him ask in faith with no doubting." We need to learn to take a posture of trust in God. I know that is difficult for many of us who are used to working things out on our own, but we need to ask God in faith and then relax, letting God work things out. I have heard it said that sometimes when we are in the heat of a battle, one of the most spiritual things we can do is take a nap. I believe that is true because it is a posture of faith and trust after we have prayed.

The Lord demands we get real with life. There is a great difference between the ideal and the real. Most of the time, life does not give us the ideal situations so we have to deal with reality. We have to learn to turn things over to God and relax. The devil wants to defeat you, but God wants to develop you. It is important to understand that we are never a failure until we quit. God's purpose is to mature us and complete us, so that we lack nothing.

TIME OUT:

1. How is your endurance? How is your attitude? Do you rejoice always?

2. Do you see how God could develop some things in your life through problems? What are they?

3. Have you learned to relax and trust God? Have you asked God for wisdom in this area?

9

PRINCIPLES FOR DECISION MAKING

Is there a Direct Command from God?

Does it Glorify God or Cause others to Stumble?

Is this Activity Necessary?

Does it Harm My Body?

Does the Activity Promote Evil?

Can I Ask God to Bless It?

PRINCIPLES OF DECISION MAKING

I have been using this outline for many years in different Bible studies that I lead. I am not sure exactly where I got it, but I believe it can help many people to make better decisions about their lives. There are many things that come up in our Christian life that we do not know whether we should be doing them or not. This outline will help you. These seven principles are important principles to consider when making decisions and commitments. We will deal with what is right and wrong when it comes to issues such as gambling, drinking, dancing, cussing and various others. It is important that you make decisions for yourself. I will try to speak only on issues I believe the Word of God covers. I will keep my opinions to myself where the Word of God is silent. I believe the problem many preachers make is trying to impose their personal opinions on people rather than preach the Word. Sometimes there are vague areas where people have to decide for themselves. Some people call these gray areas. The following principles will help us in our decision making.

Is There a Direct Command From God?

The first question we need to ask ourselves when we are about to engage in an activity is, "Do I have a direct command from God about what I am doing or what I am contemplating." 1 John 2:13 says, "I write to you, fathers, because you have known him who is from the beginning. I write to you, young men, because you have overcome the evil one. I write to you, dear children, because you have known the Father." The point is, the Bible is written for us to obey. James 1:22 says, "Do not merely listen to the word, and so deceive yourselves. Do what it says." When we see a direct command from God, it ought to stop us in our tracks. The Ten Commandments are obviously direct commands from God. "You shall not steal." "You shall not commit adultery." "You shall not give false testimony," or in other words lie. So I ask you, is there a direct command from God about cussing? Is there a direct command from God about drinking? Is there a direct command from God when it comes to gambling?

I just mentioned a few so we can test some of these areas we deal with at one time or another. The purpose for this chapter is to get you to think and pray about such areas. I definitely believe there is a direct command from God about cussing. The Bible says in Ephesians 4:29, "Do not let any unwholesome talk come out of your mouths, but only what is helpful for building others up according to their needs, that it may benefit those who listen." The Bible talks about drinking in Ephesians 5:18, "Do not get drunk on wine, which leads to debauchery. Instead be filled with the Spirit." It definitely talks about not being drunk. When it comes to an area like gambling or lotteries, certainly the Bible talks about being a good steward of the funds that God has intrusted to us. However, I do not see a direct command from God, "Thou shalt not gamble." I am not saying we should gamble, I am just saying this first principle does not give us direction on some issues we have to deal with. It does not mean we should go do these things, but the first question in our decision should be, is there a direct command from God about it?

TIME OUT:

1. Is the Bible your absolute standard for making decisions?

2. Commit to searching the Bible for answers.

Does It Glorify God Or Cause Others to Stumble?

The second test to decision making should be to ask yourself the question, "Does this activity glorify God?" 1 Corinthians 10:31 says,

"So whether you eat or drink or whatever you do, do it all for the glory of God." Ask yourself, "Does my going to a nightclub or a bar glorify God when I am in that place?" We should ask ourselves the same questions in regards to how we dress. We should ask ourselves about dancing, people we date, and about the things we put into our body. Whatever we are doing, we should ask ourselves, "Does this glorify God?" Does that activity or action bring Jesus Christ into the forefront of the minds of others, or does it somehow diminish His role in my life?

You see, these questions are for Christians. There is no reason for non-Christians to abide by these principles. It is we, who are His followers; we, who are trying to bring glory to His name, and we, who call Him Lord, who have to ask ourselves the question, "Does this glorify God?"

We have to ask ourselves another question, "Is there anything I am doing that would cause another brother to stumble?" Romans 14:21 says, "It is better not to eat meat or drink wine or to do anything else that will cause your brother to fail." In other words, an activity might be all right for you, but it is still wrong to do if it causes someone else to stumble. If it is a problem for someone else, we should stop the activity immediately–at least in their presence, so it does not become a problem for them. Romans 14:1 says, "Accept him whose faith is weak, without passing judgment on disputable matters." Verse 2 says, "One man's faith allows him to eat everything, but another man, whose faith is weak, eats only vegetables." Verse 3 says, "The man who eats everything must not look down on him who does not, and the man who does not eat everything must not condemn the man who does, for God has accepted him." Verse 4 says, "Who are you to judge someone else's servant? To his own master he stands or falls. And he will stand, for the Lord is able to make him stand." Verse 5 says, "One man considers one day more sacred than another; another man considers every day alike. Each one should be fully convinced in his own mind."

I heard a wonderful example of this from Aeneas Williams of the Arizona Cardinals. He had been sharing the Lord with another teammate and led him to the Lord. This particular teammate came from a background that does not eat meat. "It was very important," Aeneas said, "to put away those things I would normally do in order not to cause my brother to stumble." At some point, this brother may grow to where he changes his opinion on this issue. Until then, we need to be sensitive to the things we are involved in so as not to cause others to stumble.

Is This Activity Necessary?

We also must ask ourselves the question, "Is this activity necessary?" 1 Corinthians 10:23 says, "'Everything is permissible'–but not everything is beneficial. 'Everything is permissible'–but not everything is constructive." There are some things that are just not necessary. Remember, good becomes bad if it keeps you from the best. God wants the best for you and there are some activities that are not sin, but they keep you from the best.

TIME OUT:

1.   Read 1 Corinthians 10:23 and 10:31. Read Romans 14:21.

2.   Have you ever caused others to stumble by something you have said or done? If so, are you willing to stop for the sake of that person?

Does It Harm My Body?

1 Corinthians 3:16-17 says, "Don't you know that you yourselves are God's temple and that God's Spirit lives in you? If anyone destroys God's temple, God will destroy him; for God's temple is

sacred, and you are that temple." The Spirit of God lives in our body if we have made Jesus the Lord of our life. Why should we not put alcohol, drugs or tobacco into our body? Why should we work out and practice healthy eating habits? It is because our bodies are the temple of the Holy Spirit.

A survey that came out a few years ago gave the following statistics: One out of every five high school students has a drinking problem..... more than 70 percent of high school students use drugs regularly...1/3 of those who smoke marijuana began smoking it in grade school. Another survey stated that there are 11.2 million alcoholics in America and 3.3 million teenage alcoholics. It continued to say that the average drinker dies 12 years prematurely...alcohol causes 205,000 deaths annually in the United States, including over 25,000 by drunk drivers...there are 54 million smokers in America and 37 million will die prematurely...the average smoker dies nine years prematurely.... heart disease, cancer and emphysema caused by smoking, account for 300,000 deaths annually. Did you know the alcohol industry spends over $1 billion annually on advertising, and the advertising budget for Budweiser Light is $50 billion? This is more than the entire federal budget for research on alcoholism and drug abuse.

These may be shocking statistics, but these are not the reason to not do them. The reason to abstain from putting these things in our bodies is because our bodies are the temples of the Holy Spirit. The Bible says he who destroys the temple of God, God will destroy him.

TIME OUT:

1.   Do you view your body as the temple of the Holy Spirit?

2.   Read 1 Corinthians 3:16-17.

3.   What do you need to change about what you put into your body?

Does the Activity Promote Evil?

We need to ask ourselves whether the activity we are involved in or thinking about getting involved in, promotes evil. The Bible says in 1 Samuel 15:23, "For rebellion is like the sin of divination...." Even a rebellious activity can promote evil. We may not feel we are close to being involved in witchcraft, but the Bible says when we are involved in rebellious activities, defiance of parents or those in authority over us, we are promoting evil. In most circumstances, to be out late past our curfew is to be rebellious. To lie and tell our parents we are with someone when we are doing something else, is rebellion. The Bible says in Romans 12:9, "Love what must be sincere. Hate what is evil; Cling to what is good." Cling to what is good, means "to run toward it." Go after it with all you have.

What is something we should hate because it promotes evil? Music is the first thing that comes to mind. There are certain kinds of music that definitely promote evil. It may be the music we listen to that talks about rebellious activities. Activities such as shacking up with your girlfriend or boyfriend, killing cops, or anything that would promote evil instead of God's ways. If this is the case, we should stay away from that music.

Can I Ask God to Bless It?

Romans 14:23 says, "But the man who has doubts is condemned if he eats, because his eating is not from faith; and everything that does not come from faith is sin." We need to ask ourselves, "What would Jesus do in this situation?" "Can I ask God to bless this dance?" "Can I ask God to bless this relationship with this guy or gal and the activities we are going to be involved in tonight?" If we even have a problem approaching God to ask His blessing on it, we probably already have our answer.

There are many decisions that we will have to make in our lifetime. Some will be easily decided, while with others we will encounter peer pressure. If we consider these principles while making decisions in our lives, we will find they will lead us in the right direction if we have a teachable spirit. If we approach these principles with a haughty spirit, thinking we know better than God, then they will not be a benefit at all. Find the truth about these issues, and they will be a guide for us not only when we are young, but also as we make decisions in the future. Not everyone will come to the same conclusion on every issue. Keep your convictions when they are clearly stated in God's Word. Be forbearing with your opinions.

TIME OUT:

1.   Are you involved in any activity that promotes evil? If yes, get away from it quickly.

2.   Pray for God's blessing on your activities.

10

SPECIAL DAY SERMONS

Goal for the New Year
Spiritual Birthday
Death
Crucifixion
Seven Cries from the Cross
First Resurrection Words
Resurrection Voices
Thanks Must be Given
The Warfare of Christmas
What we can Learn from Christmas

Goals for the New Year

Each December I begin thinking about the New Year and what I want to accomplish. Each year my goals surround my personal character, my relationships with others, and the impact I want to have for the upcoming year. Each year the headings stay the same, but the items under the headings change. It is important to work on our personal character. We need to review the relationships we want to improve, and also decide what type of impact we want to have.

I believe our goals should always begin with our personal character because we can teach what we know, but we will always reproduce what we are. Another reason our goals should first begin with our personal character is because our relationships are hurt when our character is deficient. There is no way to have an impact if our lifestyle does not back up the words we speak. If we are impatient people, that will affect our relationships with others. To deal with our personal character is of utmost importance.

Most of us are aware of the areas in which we do not measure up to God's Word. As we start the new year, we should set some goals as to which areas, and how we want to improve ourselves. Find verses that the Lord will use in helping you change.

The second area I concentrate on each year is the area of relationships. I want to improve bad relationships and nurture the good ones. This may entail writing a letter, making a phone call, or praying to rectify a situation. All of us have enemies and all of us have relationships that are not what they should be. Make a commitment to pray about them and do what the Lord instructs. This is the key to improving our relationships. Relationships can be very enjoyable and yet they can be very frustrating. They will never improve unless we make a commitment to work on them.

I also determine how I want to improve my relationship with my wife, daughters, and those I am most committed to. Additionally, I consider the relationships God has given me so that

I am able to invest time and energy on them. I have often jokingly said, "The ministry would be fun if it was not for people." But of course, ministry IS people. Ministry IS relationships. If I am concerned about my personal character, it will also flow into the relationships I have with others.

Finally, I consider what impact I want to have this year. If my relationships and my character are not right, then I cannot have an impact. That is why we have to begin with the previous two areas before we can arrive to an area of "impact." We all want to do something for God. We all want to have an impact for God, but many times we put the cart before the horse. Our impact will flow out of our personal relationship with God and how He affects our character and relationships.

In John 15, the Bible speaks of how we will bear fruit if we abide in Him. A tree does not try to make fruit happen. It is a natural process of the tree sinking its roots down deep in the soil. A tree is known by its fruit. A Christian is also known by his or her fruit. Having an impact will happen as we abide in Christ. People will see the character of our lives and ask questions. They will see the peace of God in our hearts and will want to have a part of that peace themselves. It is great to set goals and make decisions in regards to what we are going to do for God. To really have an impact, we need to set Him as our first priority.

TIME OUT:

1. Read 2 Peter 1:5-8.

2. Write down your goals in regard to character, relationships, and impact this year.

Spiritual Birthday

The beginning of each new year, I write down new commitments for the upcoming year. On my birthday in February, I wrote down some things I have learned over the past year. I have carried this on for many years now. My spiritual birthday is in February, so it is a good time to reflect on what God has done in my life and what He has taught me over the past year. In February of 1996, I celebrated my 20th year of serving the Lord. This sermon was from 1991 when I was reflecting back on what God had taught me. I want to share with you the following 14 principles that God impressed upon my heart.

1) *God loves me.* It is very important to understand and believe this. It is a very simple concept; just like the simple song that sings, "Jesus loves me, this I know, for the Bible tells me so." We need to know He loves us when we are good and when we are bad. We need to realize we cannot earn His love. "But God demonstrates his own love for us in this: while we were still sinners, Christ died for us" (Romans 5:8). It is a condition that is stable because of His faithfulness. God's love is unconditional, but His promises are conditional. The world has that in reverse. I cannot pray, read the Word, or fast enough to make God love me any more or any less. The principles found in His Word are for my good, when I obey. Galatians 4:7 says, "So you are no longer a slave, but a son; and since you are a son, God has made you also an heir."

2) *People will not always be understanding or understood.* Some people will understand all of the time, and all of the people will understand some of the time, but all the people will not understand all the time. I have also learned that what people do not understand, they are against. Even though there are areas of misunderstanding, realize that God justifies in His time. Romans 12:19 says, "Do not take revenge, my friends, but leave rom for God's wrath, for it is written: 'It is mine to avenge; I will repay,' says the Lord." Isaiah 54:17 says, "No weapon forged against you will prevail, and you will refute every tongue that accuses you...." When you find yourself in the situation of not being understood, it is then that you need to rely on God, knowing that He justifies, and will bring all things to light in due time. We need to press on, keep silent, and even forgive others when they may not understand us or we do not understand them.

3) *Whatever you do, do for Christ first.* Colossians 3:23-24 says, "Whatever you do, work at it with all your heart, as working for the Lord, not for men, since you know that you will receive an inheritance from the Lord as a reward. It is the Lord Christ you are serving." When you do things for Christ first, rather than for other people, it takes away the wrong motives and puts the glory where it belongs. His blessings are on our efforts. Psalm 84:11 says "For the Lord God is a sun and shield; the Lord bestows favor and honor; no good thing does he withhold from those whose walk is blameless." When we do things for Christ first, we will be walking uprightly. So work for Him first, cook for Him first, teach for Him first, sing for Him first, serve Him first in everything you do.

4) *Pride is a killer.* Psalm 51:17 says, "The sacrifices of God are a broken spirit; a broken and contrite heart, O God, you will not despise." Proverbs 18:12 says, "Before his downfall a man's heart is proud, but humility comes before honor." The Bible says to humble yourself under the mighty hand of God so He may exalt you at the proper time. The test of our humility is found in our servanthood. Galatians 5:13 says, "...serve one another in love." We serve Jesus by serving others. Pride in a marriage will keep us from saying, "I'm sorry," and it will destroy that marriage. Pride in a ministry will keep us from saying, "I was wrong," and it will destroy that ministry. Pride in ourselves will destroy our relationship with the Lord. It is our job to humble ourselves and it is God's job to do the exalting. Too many times, we try to exalt ourselves and God has to do the humbling. One of the greatest ways to break down pride is to worship God. To sing to Him, to raise our hands to Him, and worship Him takes our eyes off of ourselves. This breaks down the pride of always worrying about keeping our dignity.

5) *Pain is profitable.* It polishes me. Pain keeps me seeking God. Why? Because pain produces a reaction and therefore, an end result. Isaiah 40:31 says, "But those who hope in the Lord will renew their strength. They will soar on wings like eagles; they will run and not grow weary, they will walk and not be faint." To be hoping in the Lord because of my pain is a good thing. Jesus tells

us that His power is perfected in our weakness. This is because things are done in His strength and not mine. John 3:30 says, "He must become greater; I must become less." There must be times of stretching. It means my death and His life. Psalm 119:67 says, "Before I was afflicted, I went astray but now I keep your word." Psalm 119:71 says, "It was good for me that I was afflicted so that I may learn your decrees."

6) *It is more enjoyable to be Godly than good.* I have heard it said of competition: How a man wins shows some of his character and how he loses shows it all. Proverbs 15:3 says, "The eyes of the Lord are everywhere, keeping watch on the wicked and the good." He wants our obedience rather than our sacrifice. Pursue Him and His godliness and not our own goodness. Our own goodness, the Bible says, is as "filthy rags." Proverbs 1:7 says, "The fear of the Lord is the beginning of knowledge." That is the starting point. That is where Godliness begins. The character of a man is built by what we do in secret before God. James 1:22 says, "Do not merely listen to the word, and so deceive yourselves. Do what it says."

7) *Without compassion we are nothing.* We must create a place of love, acceptance and forgiveness for people to run to in tough times. Our acceptance of people does not mean approval. We must learn to put ourselves in other people's shoes, and feel their pain. Matthew 9 says Jesus had compassion when He looked on them as sheep without a shepherd. How do you feel when someone gets a divorce, a loved one dies, a friend loses a job, or when their life is in turmoil? The answer to these questions probably shows what kind of compassion you have toward others. Without compassion our lives are not being spent on the purposes of God.

8) *When you serve God, do not expect the credit.* 1 Corinthians 3:6-9 says one waters, one plants, but God gives the increase. The Bible says no man comes to the Lord, except God's Spirit draws him. We are only tools in the hands of God, but we do not deserve the credit. The Bible says in 1 Corinthians 4, we are workers together with the Lord. We need to understand that God is in control, and it is dangerous to expect a pat on the back. Do not misunderstand me, we all need a pat on the back, but we should not expect it.

9) *God's wisdom can save us from having to learn through experience.* I have learned that to obtain favor, wisdom, and courage in my life, I read Psalms and Proverbs every day. It does not take that long, but it is amazing the wisdom you will gain. 1 Corinthians 15:33 says bad company corrupts good morals. Now, you can either learn that through experience, or you can learn it by obeying God. Too many of us learn through experience when we could have circumvented some situations by obeying God's Word first. We can learn through wisdom about the way God wants us to handle our finances. It says in Malachi 3:8, "Will a man rob God? Yet you rob me. But you ask, 'How do we rob you?'" Ed Cole writes in his book, Communication, Sex, and Money, "You can pray until you are blue in the face, but you can never get back through the sacrifice of prayer, what you have already lost through disobedience." We can learn the wisdom we need to be a good husband from 1 Peter 3:7: "Husbands, in the same way be considerate as you live with your wives, and treat them respect as the weaker partner and as heirs with you of the gracious gift of life, so that nothing will hinder your prayers." Putting God's Word into practice can keep us from having to go through the school of hard knocks.

10) *The key is prayer.* Psalm 118:6 says, "The Lord is with me! I will not be afraid. What can man do to me?" We need to understand that God is on our side even when life is not going the way we want it to. We must persevere even in our prayer life. Things do not always happen quickly. I know I prayed for my family for 10 years before I started seeing some of the results of my prayers. We have seen my Mom and Dad's marriage restored. I have seen my whole family give their hearts to Jesus, even when it seemed like my prayers were bouncing off the walls. 1 Corinthians 15:58 says, "Therefore, my dear brothers, stand firm. Let nothing move you. Always give yourselves fully to the work of the Lord, because you know that your labor in the Lord is not in vain." We need to know that our toiling for the Lord is not in vain. Hebrews 10:23-25 says, "Let us hold unswervingly to the hope we profess, for he who promised is faithful. And let us consider how we may spur one

another on toward love and good deeds. Let us not give up meeting together, as some are in the habit of doing, but let us encourage one another–and all the more as you see the Day approaching."

11) *To be led by the Spirit is the key to all of life.* You cannot always go by your circumstances. What if Satan was involved in the circumstances? You should not be led by your flesh, because your flesh goes its own direction. You should not be led by your mind, because the enemy might plant seeds in your mind. Proverbs 20:27 says, "The lamp of the Lord searches the spirit of a man; it searches out his inmost being." In John 10:27 it says, "My sheep listen to my voice; I know them, and they follow me." Isaiah 30:21 says, "Whether you turn to the right or to the left, your ears will hear a voice behind you, saying, 'This is the way; walk in it!'" The Spirit's leading will never violate the Word of God. John 6:63 says, "The Spirit gives life; the flesh counts for nothing. The words I have spoken to you are spirit and they are life." The Spirit works in cooperation with the Word of God.

12) *We must apply, but not pervert God's holy principles.* Everything God does, He does according to a pattern and it is based on a principle. God gives principles for leadership in 2 Timothy. He said, entrust to faithful men whom God will then make able. The perversion of the principles would be to give to ABLE people and then ask God to make them faithful. Our endeavors should be built on consistency and faithfulness. God commits to character, not talent. We will be judged by our faithfulness, not our bigness. That is why one of the principles is to trust things to faithful men and not talented men. David was chosen by Samuel because Samuel was not looking on the outward appearance, but looking on the heart. God looks on our hearts.

Then there is the principle of faith. The Bible says that Abraham called those things which were not as though they were. The perversion is to call those things which are as though they are not. Some people try to say we are never supposed to be sick, or admit we are sick. That is calling those things that ARE as though they are not. That is perversion and an error. Error is, many times, truth carried to the extreme. We must learn to do all things in moderation.

13) *Certain things will remain a mystery.* Why this child died or what God's will was in a certain situation will sometimes remain a mystery. The Bible tells us that God's ways are higher than our ways. I have to chalk things up to "someday" He will give me answers for some of the questions I have. Some things will always remain a mystery while I am still on this earth. We do not have to have an answer for everything that happens here. One day we will see things clearly, and we will be able to talk to Jesus about the questions we had.

14) *Some things are not that important.* I have heard the story about little Joey spilling his milk all the time at the dinner table and his parents getting upset. The same boy was killed by a car backing out of a driveway. Now, how little Joey's parents wished Joey was around to spill the milk like he used to do. It is just a reminder that we get upset about the smallest things and let them destroy the things that matter the most to us. I am starting to learn more and more that some things are not that big of a deal. They really are not that big of an issue at all.

TIME OUT:

1.   Write down some of the spiritual lessons God has taught you this past year. Take your time and do not rush it.

Death

I read an article in Sports Illustrated about all the athletes who died in 1993. It was a tragic year for the sports world. As I thumbed through that Sports Illustrated, I was reminded of how fragile life is. I saw pictures of Drazen Petrovich and Reggie Lewis from the NBA and a couple of college athletes who died in automobile accidents. The sports world was stunned when Arthur Ashe made his tragic announcement and died only a few months later. The suicide of Jeff Alm from the Houston Oilers caught us all by surprise, along with the deaths of auto racers Davey Allison and Allen Kulwicki. The boating accidents of the Cleveland Indians pitchers, Tim Cruz and Steve Ohlen, left the Indians organization in complete shock. We lost Jim Valvano, the North Carolina State basketball coach to his fight with cancer. Dave Warner of the L.A. Raiders lost his life after ingesting cocaine. Those of us in Arizona were certainly saddened by the death of LPGA player Heather Farr.

As I was sitting there, I decided that we need to discuss the subject of death. None of us has knowledge of what will happen in the course of a year. In the New Testament, James says life is but a vapor. We appear for a while and then we are gone. We need to be ready for death. Hebrews 9:27 says, "Just as man is destined to die once, and after that to face judgment."

I was not looking forward to conducting a chapel service on death. As I drove to the America West Arena, I prayed the Lord would give me something else to speak on. Death was definitely the subject God laid on my heart. Shortly after praying that prayer, I looked up and there was a cemetery. I believe it was a confirmation that this was the subject I was to speak on. As I began the chapel, one of the players stopped me to ask if I had heard about the father of one of the Suns' employees who had a fatal accident the evening before. It was certainly another confirmation for this topic. I told the players that night, that if you are born once, you will die twice. But if you are born twice, you will only die once. If Jesus comes again before we die, we will not have to die even once.

In other words, if we are only born physically, we will die both physically and spiritually. If we give our hearts to Christ and are born again, born a second time, then we will only die once (physically). The Bible says in 1 Corinthians 15:55, "Where, O death, is your victory? Where, O death, is your sting?" To know Christ, is to take away the sting of death. The Bible says in 2 Corinthians 5:8, "We are confident, I say, and would prefer to be away from the body and at home with the Lord." Death is a one way ticket home for a Christian. It is a better place. More so than we can even comprehend. The key is to be ready.

I have presided over two funerals in my ministry. One was for a young boy who had just accepted the Lord the day before. At the funeral we offered an opportunity for the people there to accept Christ and about 25 responded. Death makes us reflect on what is really important in life. Too many times we feel invincible, and the death of someone we care about suddenly reminds us we are not.

The other funeral was for a lady who was in her seventies. We spoke of how we wanted to celebrate her life and her going home to be with the Lord. As a Christian, we can celebrate others going home because they are in a better place. Those of us left behind are the ones who grieve. If they are born again and we also are born again, we know we will be with them again some day. If we are ready to meet the Lord, we can celebrate their life and their home going even in the midst of death.

What should our response be to those who have lost a loved one? I believe we can turn to 1 Thessalonians 4:13-18 for our response. Verse 13 says, "Brothers, we do not want you to be ignorant about those who fall asleep, or to grieve like the rest of men, who have no hope. We believe that Jesus died and rose again and so we believe that God will bring with Jesus those who have fallen asleep in him. According to the Lord's own word, we tell you that we who are still alive, who are left till the coming of the Lord, will certainly not precede those who have fallen asleep. For the Lord himself will come down from heaven, with a loud command, with the voice of the archangel and with the trumpet call of God, and the dead in Christ will rise first. After that, we who are still alive and are left will be caught up together with them in the clouds to meet the Lord in the air. And so we will be with the Lord forever. Therefore encourage each other with these words."

I believe these verses should be read at every Christian's funeral. The Bible tells us to comfort and encourage each other with these words. It also tells us to rejoice with those who rejoice and weep with those who weep. I believe we are to bear their burdens and to feel their sorrow. However, I also believe we can proclaim the Good News; Death is not a tragic thing for a Christian, but a home going.

TIME OUT:

1.   Are you ready to die? Read 1 Thessalonians 4:13-18.

2.   Help get as many people ready for death as possible by telling them the Good News of Jesus Christ.

The Crucifixion

Have you really considered what happened on Good Friday? Jesus Christ took the sins of the world upon His own body while on the cross. He had been through several mock trials, which proclaimed Him guilty of claiming to be God. Pilate said he found "no wrong in this man." Pilate asked, "Who should I release, Barabbas or Jesus?" The crowd cried to release Barabbas and crucify Jesus. In addition to all of the mental torment Jesus went through, there was also much physical suffering. Many churches have theatrical productions during the week of Easter. I encourage you to attend one, as they portray what Jesus went through on that day and week for us.

He first had to carry his 90-pound cross up the mountain after He went through the Roman scourge. A whip with pieces of metal, bone, and lead attached to the lashes, was pulled from the top of His back to the bottom. Roman law stated 40 lashes could not be exceeded on any one person. Because of strict adherence of the law by the Sanhedrin, they inflicted 39 lashes, leaving room for a miscount. After all this, we see our Lord carrying His cross to Calvary.

Next, we see Jesus with spikes being driven, not through the palm of his hands, but through His wrists. A big spike is then driven through the middle of both legs near the ankles. Of course, before they put Him on the cross they placed a crown of thorns on the brow of His head, causing immense pain and bleeding. From the jolt of dropping the cross into the hole in the ground, His shoulders most likely separated. In order to keep from suffocating, He had to keep pushing His body upward to grasp a breath while He was on the cross. When He requested water, they handed Him vinegar. There were two thieves on the crosses next to Jesus, one on each side. One thief mocked Jesus saying, "If you are really the Christ, save yourself and save us." The other thief then rebuked him for what he said to Jesus, saying, "Don't you see that we are both in the same judgment, but this man Jesus, has done nothing wrong." He then looked across to Jesus and said, "Lord when you come again into your kingdom, remember me." Jesus then replied, "Today, you shall be with me in Paradise." This was because the thief recognized Jesus as the one God sent to be the Savior of the world. Because he had a repentant heart, called Him Lord, and trusted Him with his soul, Jesus told him he would spend eternity in heaven.

Probably worst of all, was when the Father had to turn His back on His Son. 2 Corinthians 5:21 says, "God made him who had no sin to be sin for us, so that in him we might become the righteousness of God." Jesus actually became sin on the cross. The Father had to turn His back on the sin and His Son. Jesus then cried out, "Lord, Lord, why hast thou forsaken me?" But the Father did not forsake Him, He raised Him up from the dead. This is when the sky turned black and the veil of the curtain was torn in two from top to bottom. Jesus cried out, "It is finished" and breathed His last breath. Even after He was dead, they put a spear in His side to ensure His death. Out came blood and water and met in a pool at the foot of the cross. In Hebrews 9:22, God said without the shedding of blood, there is no forgiveness of sin. Yet, He did this because He loved us. In Isaiah it tells us that God the Father will see the travail of His Christ's soul and will be satisfied. It pleased God to bruise Him. God needed a blood sacrifice for the forgiveness of our sins. Jesus took our place. He wanted us to spend eternity with Him, and the only way for us to find forgiveness of our sin was for Him to take our place on the cross. Sin had to be dealt with, and Jesus dealt with it for us on the cross.

Next time you take communion and remember the blood of our Lord Jesus Christ, think of what He went through for you. Isaiah 53:5-6 says, "But he was pierced for our transgressions, he was crushed for our iniquities; the punishment that brought us peace was upon him, and by his wounds we are healed. We all, like sheep, have gone astray, each of us has turned to his own way; and the Lord has laid on him the iniquity of us all." What Jesus went through for us is awesome. Let us never take it for granted.

God is satisfied when we, with our faith, accept him as Lord and Savior. Jesus pleased God when he became the sacrificial Lamb.

TIME OUT:

1.   Go to an Easter production that portrays what Jesus went through for us.

2.   Spend some time thanking Jesus for what He went through for you.

Seven Cries from the Cross

In Galatians 2:20, "I have been crucified with Christ and I no longer live, but Christ lives in me. The life I live in the body, I live by faith in the Son of God, who loved me and gave himself for me." Jesus Christ's sacrifice on the cross is the key to our forgiveness of sins. The Bible says that without the shedding of blood, there is no remission of sins. 2 Corinthians 5:21 says that Jesus was our substitute on the cross. He took on our sin and we took on His righteousness. What Jesus said on the cross has great significance to us as Christians. We need to pay particular attention to the words He spoke while hanging on the cross. He said what He did for a reason. If applied to our lives, these words can make a great difference in the way we view our lives. Let's look at the seven statements He made while on the cross.

1. "Father forgive them." Luke 23:34 says, "Jesus said, 'Father, forgive them, for they do not know what they are doing.' And they divided up his clothes by casting lots." Even while they were mocking and ridiculing Him, and telling Him to get down if He really was the son of God, Jesus had compassion on them. He remembered His purpose for being on the cross. The Bible says it is God's will that none perish, no not one. Jesus cared for all people. He has turned around and given us the same mission. We need to love others, accept them, and forgive them as Christ has done. Our acceptance of others does not mean approval of everything they do. If people do not know we accept them, they will never confide in us or come to us in their times of need. One of my favorite quotes is from Josh McDowell, "Rules without relationship leads to rebellion."

I think one of the greatest testimonies is that of Bobby Richardson at Mickey Mantle's funeral. There was a wild bunch in the New York Yankees heyday–Mickey Mantle, Whitey Ford and Billy Martin. Bobby Richardson was one of the few Christians on the team. Yet it was Bobby Richardson who got a call from Mickey when he was facing death, and Bobby Richardson led Mickey to the Lord. They respected Bobby Richardson's lifestyle.

Remember that Jesus was crucified at the end of His ministry, and it was the equivalent of the local ministerial association that put Him on the cross. The religious community may put you on the cross too. People are so quick to judge these days. We all tend to judge others by what they do, and ourselves, by our intentions. Legalism is a false religion. We need to simply and plainly love people.

I love a song I heard a few months ago that said, "Don't shoot the wounded. Someday you might be one." Never labor under the misconception that acceptance breeds license. To the contrary, your very acceptance of a brother will make him strong. Others will not be confused when it comes to questions of right and wrong if our teaching and personal lifestyle establish clear standards. For example, a person who uses profanity is not going to imagine you approve of such language just because you accept him personally. As he hears your reverent speech and learns God's Word, and most importantly comes to love God, he will understand clearly that profanity is wrong. But if you communicate personal rejection to someone, he will never stay around long enough to be touched by God through you. Romans 5:8 says, "God demonstrates his own love for us in this: While we were still sinners, Christ died for us."

Another example of accepting people would be having a divorce recovery group in your church. You are not promoting divorce, you are trying to fix something that is already broken. The church of Jesus Christ is similar to a hospital. We try to help mend broken hearts. Too many people these days run to the bar to share their problems rather than run to the church for acceptance. Jesus said, "Father, forgive them for they know not what they do." As He looked down on the people who nailed Him to the cross, He still forgave them. We need to be forgiving people. We cannot allow resentment, hate and bitterness to fester in our lives. We need to extend the grace of God that has been extended to us.

2. "I thirst." John 19:28 says, "...Jesus said, 'I am thirsty.'" I know this is referring to a physical thirst, but we can learn a spiritual principle. We need to be thirsty for the kingdom of God. In Matthew chapter 5, it says that those who hunger and thirst for righteousness will be filled. Psalm 63:1-2 says, "Oh God, you are my God, earnestly I seek you; my soul thirsts for you, my body longs for you, in a dry and weary land where there is no water." Many today try to quench their spiritual thirst with drugs, sex, money and fame. The only way to solve our spiritual thirst is to seek God. Another point concerning Jesus' thirst on the cross, is that it shows His humanity. The Bible says that He was in all ways tempted like us, and yet without sin. When we get thirsty, hungry, and tired, we many times give in to temptation, but Jesus never did.

3. "Woman, behold thy son." John 19:26 says, "When Jesus

saw his mother there, and the disciple whom He loved standing nearby, he said to his mother, 'Dear woman, here is your son,' and to the disciple, 'Here is your mother.' From that time on, this disciple took her into his home." Jesus gave up those closest to Him because He was about to go back and be with His Father, but He was still tending to the needs of those He cared for. He made sure they were taken care of. Jesus lived His life for others. 1 Timothy 5:8 says, "If anyone does not provide for his relatives, and especially for his immediate family, he has denied the faith and is worse than an unbeliever. Our first ministry should be to our family members, friends and neighbors whom God has strategically placed in our lives.

4. "My God, my God, why hast thou forsaken me?" Matthew 27:46 says that Jesus said, "My God, my God, why have you forsaken me?" This was spoken after the ninth hour when darkness had overcome the earth. Jesus, at this point, felt the separation from His Father because of the sin offering He had become. The Father had actually turned his back on His son because He could not look upon the sin that Jesus had become. Jesus did not sin Himself, but He became our sin offering in order to bring us forgiveness and redemption. The Father actually never forsook Him, but Jesus felt the separation that sin creates. He was there all the time, but that is what sin does—it creates a chasm, a gulf, a separation in our relationship with God. We need to quickly repent and ask God to forgive us when we sin, so we can get back in right standing with God. James 4:8 says, "Come near to God and He will come near to you...." 1 John 1:9 says, "If we confess our sins, he is faithful and just and will forgive us our sins and purify us from all unrighteousness." Adam and Eve ran and hid when they recognized their sin. We need to run to God and confess our sin and get back in that right relationship with Him.

5. "Today you shall be with me in paradise." Luke 23:43 says, "Jesus answered him, 'I tell you the truth, today you will be with me in paradise.'" One thief hurled insults at Him, saying, "If you are the Christ, save yourself." But the other criminal rebuked him saying,

"Don't you fear God?" and said, "Lord remember me when you come into your kingdom." Jesus said, "I tell you the truth, today you will be with me in paradise." Jesus was a soul winner to the last drop of blood. We need to be soul winners also. This illustrates the point that it is grace and grace alone by which we are saved. This man did not come down off the cross and get baptized. He didn't do anything but believe in Jesus Christ and repent of his sins and wrong ways. It was his attitude and receiving Christ on the cross to which Jesus said, "Today you will be with me in paradise." Many rely on their good works to save them. Ephesians 2:8-9 says, "For it is by grace you have been saved, through faith– and this not of yourselves, it is the gift of God–and not by works, so that no one can boast."

6. "It is finished." In John 19:30 Jesus said, "It is finished." With that, He bowed His head and gave up His Spirit. We need to understand that Christianity is a "done" religion. Cease from your struggling and understand our relationship with Him is based on what He has done and not on what we have done. When we realize that "it is finished" and He has provided all that needs to be provided for our salvation, we will cease from our struggling to gain God's approval. We gain God's approval by receiving His gift of Jesus Christ on the cross. He has provided everything for our salvation. We will constantly be in bondage if we relate to God on the basis of what we do. We need to relate to God on the basis of His gift and sacrifice of Jesus on the cross.

7. "Into Thy hands I commit my spirit." Luke 23:46 says, "Jesus called out with a loud voice, 'Father, into your hands I commit my spirit.' When he had said this, he breathed His last." It is important to know that God has a plan for your life. It is also important to understand that God is in control. We need to constantly yield to the will of the Father. John 15:5 says He is the vine and we are the branches. Romans 6:11, "In the same way, count yourselves dead to sin but alive to God in Christ Jesus." In verse 13 it says, "Do not offer the parts of your body to sin, as instruments of wickedness, but rather offer yourselves to God as

those who have been brought from death to life; and offer the parts of your body to him as instruments of righteousness." Just as Jesus said, "Into thy hands I commit my spirit," we need to say to God, "Lord, I am yours and I yield myself to you for your purpose." It is all about what Christ can get out of it, not what we can get out of it. To live our lives for ourselves is selfish. To yield ourselves to Him on a daily basis is to live our lives for God's glory. Then it is no longer I, but Christ living His life through us, just as God lived His life through Christ when He walked on earth. Anything else is just religion, not Christianity.

First Resurrection Words

In John chapter 20, we are told the story of the resurrection. You will hear this story referred to on many Easter Sundays. The words spoken in this chapter are words of life, encouragement, joy, hope, comfort, and love. We will look at some of the first words spoken after the resurrection. The resurrection is what sets apart Christianity from every other religion. Let's discuss those first words spoken that Easter Sunday morning.

1. "Whom do you seek?" John 20:15 says, "Jesus said to her, 'Woman, why are you weeping? Whom are you seeking?' She supposing Him to be the gardener, said to Him, 'Sir, if you have carried Him away, tell me where you have laid Him and I will take Him away.'" Mary Magdalene missed Him. She longed for Him. While Peter and John were not seeking Him, she was weeping and looking in the tomb. She was diligently seeking Him. He was there all the time, although she did not recognize Him. Jesus asked her, "Whom are you seeking?" That is a sermon in and of itself. The Bible says in Jeremiah 29:13, "If you seek me with all of your heart, you will surely find me." Are we seeking Jesus with all of our heart? Are we looking and longing for Him, or are we like Peter and John who were not looking for Him at all?

2. "Peace be unto you." John 20:19 says, "On the evening of

that first day of the week, when the disciples were together, with the doors locked for fear of the Jews, Jesus came and stood among them and said, 'Peace be with you!'" Notice it states the doors were shut for fear of the Jews. Their hearts were trembling. They were even fearing for their lives. Their hopes and dreams had been shattered by the one they thought to be the Savior, the Messiah. All of a sudden, Jesus presented Himself and said, "Peace be unto you." Jesus comforts our broken, hurting hearts today as well. I like the song that sings, "He may not be there when you want Him, but He's always right on time." Jesus seems to show up when we need Him most, and says, "Peace be unto you." Because we serve a risen Savior, He comes and brings peace today just as He did many years ago. One of the greatest needs we have in our lives today, is the need for peace. With the stress that many people face today, they need peace. Jesus said in Matthew 11:28-30, "Come to me, all you who are weary and burdened, and I will give you rest. Take my yoke upon you and learn from me, for I am gentle and humble in heart and you will find rest for your souls. For my yoke is easy and my burden is light." Jesus Christ can bring peace to weary souls today.

3.   "Why are you so sad?" In Luke 24:17, they did not know who Jesus was when He said to them, "What are you discussing together as you walk along? They stood still, their faces downcast." It seemed like all was lost. Once again, Jesus was there all the time. They just did not recognize Him. The Bible says in 1 Peter 5:7 that we can cast all of our cares upon Him because He cares for us. There is no doubt that life sometimes makes us sad. When things do not go the way we want them to go, it can seem like all is lost. Ask yourself why Jesus asked the question, "Why are you so sad?" He was trying to bring hope to that situation. He was saying, "I am here even in the midst of your problems. You may think I am not here, but I am." This is why Paul wrote "Rejoice in the Lord always, again, I say rejoice," in Philippians 4:4. In another portion of scripture He said, "Be of good cheer." He also said to count it all joy when you encounter trials of many kinds and to let not your hearts

be troubled. I believe Jesus shows up and says, "Why are you so sad? I am here. I want to make a difference. There is hope, even in the middle of the storms of life."

4. "Put your finger here, see my hands. Reach out your hand and put it into my side. Stop doubting and believe." Jesus said that in John 20:27. It was as if Jesus knew that Thomas HAD to know whether his Lord was alive or not. He knew Thomas' frail frame. Jesus knew he needed extra assurance. Jesus was willing to meet him right where he was, and wanted to prove himself to Thomas. The fact that these were some of His first actions and first words spoken after the resurrection, shows His willingness to meet each of us where we are in our spiritual journey. God is willing to reveal Himself. God is willing to prove Himself to us. At the same time, in John 20:29 He says, "…blessed are those who have not seen and yet have believed." He is telling us that He is willing to meet Thomas where he is, as well as, I am going to be with those who have not experienced what Thomas has.

5. "Receive the Holy Spirit." The Holy Spirit had not yet been given when He spoke these words in John 20:22. This is the first in-filling of the Holy Spirit. It is when the Spirit of God actually started taking up residence in the life of a believer. When the Bible says we can have an abundant life, it is because of God's Spirit dwelling in these fleshly bodies. In 2 Corinthians 4:7 it says, "But we have this treasure in jars of clay to show that this all-surpassing power is from God and not from us." The treasure we have is the Holy Spirit. We need to be continually filled with the Holy Spirit. Ephesians 5 says be filled with the Spirit. We need a fresh anointing daily, or our spiritual lives can get stale. The Bible says if anyone has not the Spirit of God, then he does not belong to God." We need to ask God to continually fill our cup. These first resurrection words are important because apart from the Spirit of God, we have nothing to give. John 6:63 says, "The Spirit gives life; the flesh counts for nothing. The words I have spoken to you are spirit and they are life." Zechariah 4:6 says, "…Not by might nor by power, but by my Spirit…."

6. "Feed my sheep." In John 21:15-19 Jesus said, "...Feed my sheep...." He was asking John if he really loved Him. John said, "...Yes, Lord, you know that I love you...." Three times Jesus said to take care of my lambs or feed my sheep. Jesus was telling John that the proof of your love for me will be your caring for my sheep. Sheep are the followers of Jesus Christ. Ephesians 4:29 says we are to edify one another. Hebrews 3:13 says, "But encourage one another daily, as long as it is called Today, so that none of you may be hardened by sin's deceitfulness." John 13:35 says, "By this all men will know that you are my disciples, if you love one another." 2 Timothy 4:2-3 says, "Preach the Word; be prepared in season and out of season; correct, rebuke and encourage—with great patience and careful instruction. For the time will come when men will not put up with sound doctrine. Instead, to suit their own desires, they will gather around them a great number of teachers to say what their itching ears want to hear." All of these are a part of feeding God's sheep. Encouraging people, loving people, edifying people and speaking the truth of God to people. It is not easy, yet it is what God wants us to do.

7. "Tarry in the City of Jerusalem." Jesus spoke these words in Luke 24:49 when He told His disciples to wait for the Holy Spirit. This was before He ascended into heaven. He said, "I am going to send you what my Father has promised; but stay in the city until you have been clothed with power from on high." Acts 1:8 says, "But you will receive power when the Holy Spirit comes on you; and you will be my witnesses in Jerusalem, and in all Judea and Samaria, and to the ends of the earth." If they had not waited for the Spirit of God, they would not have been clothed from that power from on high. Too many times we are too busy to take time for God. There is a barrenness that happens in our busy lives. The only way we will get the power we need to live this Christian life is to wait on God.

Some of the first words Jesus spoke after He arose from the dead were to "tarry" or "wait." We must be people who wait on the Lord. We need to learn to wait on Him daily. We need a fresh touch from God each day.

8. "So send I you." John 20:21 says, "...Peace be with you! As the Father has sent me, I am sending you." He told his disciples to "go, be his witnesses." Matthew 28:18 says, "...All authority in heaven and on earth has been given to me. Therefore go and make disciples of all nations, baptizing them in the name of the Father and of the Son and of the Holy Spirit, and teaching them to obey everything I have commanded you. And surely I am with you always, to the very end of the age." We are called to go and be his witnesses. He said as He was sent from the Father, He is now sending us to win the lost for Him. He said He will go with us because only His Spirit, drawing men to Himself, really changes people's hearts. God always uses an instrument or a vessel to flow through. Isn't it interesting that some of the first resurrection words were those stating that He is sending us to a lost and dying world? There are so many people in need of Jesus Christ, and if He has touched our hearts, then we must believe He wants to touch others as well. These first resurrection words are a great help in understanding what Jesus wants to do in our lives, but also how He wants to use each of us. Because of the resurrection, we can now live a resurrected, overcoming life. Galatians 2:20 says, "I have been crucified with Christ and I no longer live, but Christ lives in me. The life I live in the body, I live by faith in the Son of God, who loved me and gave himself for me." It is because of the resurrection that Jesus spoke these words and it is because of the resurrection that we can live out these words in our daily lives.

TIME OUT:

1. Do you wait on God regularly? We need to be regularly filled with His Spirit to be effective for Him!

2. Where is God sending you to be His witness?

3. Is the peace of God evident in your life? If not, why?

Resurrection Voices

All that Jesus said stands or falls, based on the resurrection. 1 Corinthians 15:17 says, "And if Christ has not been raised, your faith is futile; you are still in your sins." The resurrection of Jesus Christ is the most powerful voice of Christianity.

All of earth's religions must bow before the tremendous truth and voice of the resurrection of Jesus Christ. The founders of their religions are dead and no longer can influence those who are living. The voice of Jesus Christ rings throughout the world, bringing hope, peace, and life. What did the resurrection mean to those first followers of Jesus Christ?

First, the resurrection was a voice of victory. Matthew 28:10 says Jesus told His disciples to go into Galilee. Galilee, to them, meant defeat. Galilee meant to be mocked. The people would say, "Where is your King? Where is your Savior?" But Christ told them he would go before them into Galilee. This was a voice of glorious assurance. In the resurrection of Christ, there is guaranteed victory for those who put their trust in Him. I think it is a good idea for each of us to wake up each morning and put on the full armor of God, and walk ourselves through this process to remind us who our enemy is, and what we have to do to defeat him. But the greatest reason we will win is because He is alive.

Secondly, the resurrection is a voice of faith. When Thomas saw his Savior nailed to the cross, then laid in the tomb, his rational mind could only conceive that this was the end. Then three days later he heard from his friends that Jesus was alive. It was a taunting thing. He said in John 20:25, "...Unless I see the nail marks in his hands and put my finger where the nails were, and put my hand into his side, I will not believe it."

When Thomas heard His voice, saw the nail prints where He had been nailed to the cross, and beheld the glorious resurrected Christ, he cried, "My Lord and my God." The resurrection gave faith to Thomas. I have often said, "If Jesus Christ can be raised from the dead in bodily form, He can raise any marriage or any situation from the dead as well." The resurrection is a voice of faith.

Thirdly, the resurrection is a voice of forgiveness. After He had risen, we read of the angels speaking before the Lord saying, "Go tell my disciples and Peter." (Mark 16:7) Christ's last look at Peter before He died was one of great sorrow. Christ was looking upon the one who had backslidden by cursing and denying Him with his own lips. Peter had stood before the common people of his time and declared he did not even know Jesus. Peter probably wondered if he could ever be loved by the Lord again. But Christ knew his heart and the resurrection became a voice of forgiveness for Peter. Jesus not only asked for His disciples, but also very specifically, wanted Peter. There is no doubt that these were the happiest words Simon Peter ever heard. He knew for sure he was included once again with the disciples. Peter was absolutely forgiven for his backslidden condition. How beautiful that the resurrection is also a voice of forgiveness.

Fourthly, the resurrection is a voice of encouragement. Read the story in Luke 24:13-35 of when the disciples were walking with Jesus. Cleopas and his friends were very sad. They spoke of the great calamity that had befallen the world when the Savior was crucified. Christ joined the pathetic, discouraged group and began to explain what it truly meant. At the same time, Christ shielded His identity from them. They even broke bread in the home of Cleopas. That is where Christ gave the revelation of Himself. They said, "Did not our hearts burn within us?" The two, so full of their new found joy, ran from their home into the streets and into the homes of those they knew shouting, "The Lord is risen indeed." Easter is a voice of encouragement.

Finally, the resurrection is a voice of joy. Mary Magdalene was a fallen woman who had seven spirits cast out of her. She became so attached to Christ, she followed Him wherever He went to minister. She was even at the cross when Christ died, and three mornings later she was standing at the tomb when He arose. Mary was looking for Christ. She was longing for Him. She was very sorrowful when she saw that the tomb was empty. She asked one whom she supposed to be the gardener, "Where have you laid Him?" The Lord Jesus turned and spoke the first resurrection words to her, "Woman, why are you crying?" (John 20:15). Great joy flooded her life, and she, more than any other, believed the voice of joy that Easter brings.

TIME OUT:

1.   Read Revelation 1:18 and 1 Corinthians 15:17.

2.   Read the full story of the Lord's resurrection in Matthew 28 and Luke 24.

Thanks Must Be Given

A thankful heart is the key to growth in the Lord and a prevention for backsliding. Being thankful keeps us in a position of dependence upon God. It keeps us from feeling self-reliant. Thankfulness produces humility. 1 Thessalonians 5:18 says, "Give thanks in all circumstances, for this is God's will for you in Christ Jesus." Psalm 103 says forget none of the Lord's benefits. When you taste that the Lord is good, and you remember His benefits, you will not want to go back to your former way of living. You are constantly reminded of God's goodness and all He has done for you. You will not want to settle for anything less. 2 Timothy 3:1-9 says unthankfulness is a sign of the times.

Psalm 103 reminds us of some of the benefits the Lord has given us. Verse 3 says He "forgives all your sins and heals all your diseases." I believe we all should not only be aware, but thankful daily for the forgiveness God provides. What an awesome God we have, one we can run to in times of sickness. Verse 4 says He "redeems your life from the pit and crowns you with love and compassion." Verse 5 says He "satisfies your desires with good things so that your youth is renewed like the eagle's." Verse 10 says He does not treat us as our sins deserve. Be thankful people, not only for the benefits, but also for the goodness God has bestowed upon us. In being thankful, we are in closer communion with God, therefore, thankfulness can be a prevention for backsliding.

We need to cultivate thankfulness with God, our spouse, friends and teammates, showing appreciation toward the people who do things for us. We can cultivate this thankfulness with a smile, a handshake, a phone call, letter, hug, or kind deed. As we cultivate this thankfulness toward the people we are surrounded by, we will view them, and God in a different way. We also will be constantly reminded of what God has done for us.

I heard a Pastor once state in a sermon, "Thanksgiving is not Thanksgiving unless thanks are given." It must be verbalized with your mouth. Thanksgiving is something that is expressed to God or to others.

Hebrews 13:15 says, "...let us continually offer to God the sacrifice of praise–the fruit of lips that confess his name." We are to use our lips to thank and praise His name continually!

What can we thank God for? James 1:17 says, "Every good and perfect gift is from above...." Therefore, we can thank Him for family, friends, health, jobs, food, clothing, houses and even life itself. They all come from Him. Most importantly, we should not forget to thank Him for the salvation He provided for us on the cross.

Remember the 10 lepers that were healed in Luke 17:11-17? Only one returned to say thank you. Nine went on their way, probably with gratefulness in their heart, but never taking time to express how thankful they were. Jesus had forever changed their lives from this dreaded disease, and yet no thanks were given.

The Psalmist, David, wrote in Psalm 34:8, "Taste and see that the Lord is good...." Once you have tasted the goodness of God, you never want to go back. Keep tasting the goodness of God.
Let us stir up thankfulness among us, to God and others.

Remember, Thanksgiving is only Thanksgiving when thanks are given.

TIME OUT:

1.   Read James 1:17, Hebrews 13:15 and 1 Thessalonians 5:18.

2.   Have you ever taken time to thank your mom and dad for your upbringing?

3.   Write a letter to the Lord expressing all of the things for which you are thankful.

4.   Read Psalm 103. Is thankfulness in your heart and on your lips toward others? Have you really stopped to thank God for your spouse, for your food, for your clothing and shelter?

The Warfare of Christmas

The Christmas story is a wonderful one, but it also has a down side as well. Just as with each great miracle of God, there is a devilish plot to stop Jesus from His proposed purpose. The Messiah had come to take away the sins of the world by dying on the cross. The devil tries to stop the plan of God, and accomplish his own mission through people. In this particular case, it was through King Herod (Luke chapter 2). This was an obvious attempt by the devil to snuff out the purpose of Jesus' life before He had time to develop. King Herod ordered that all boys under the age of two years old be killed. So it is today, there is an attack on children like never before. The devil, working through feminist groups, pro-pornography groups, gay activists and abortionist, have targeted children to market their cause. I know this is not politically correct, but still true.

   Pornography targets their material to children 11 to 13 years of age. The reason? Money. Get them hooked at a young age and they will be hooked for life. Destroy the children to make a buck. Little do they realize that rape, incest, filthy minds, abuse, molestation, abduction and women viewed as sexual objects, are the result. I would say there is a warfare being staged against our children.

The gay activist groups have developed a curriculum for the public school system beginning in the first grade that perpetrates their lifestyle. In New York and other states, there are groups fighting these curriculums. Targeting little six-year-old minds with a lifestyle that is anti-God is definitely warring for our children. Those who oppose their ideology and values get labeled as intolerant and bigots, but we must stand for the truth and understand the battle.

The issue of abortion describes this warfare like no other. The devil would love to not only steal, but destroy the life of a child before it ever begins. He has been successful in killing over 20 million babies since 1973, the year abortion was legalized. If the devil used people in the days of King Herod, he will use the same tool today to fulfill his purpose against children. It is even legal in America to kill babies in the third trimester, even to the point of delivery! How ludicrous!

The Bible has verses to prove how much of a person an unborn baby really is. In Luke 1:44, Elizabeth said the baby in her womb leaped for joy when she heard Mary's greeting. The baby responded to Mary's voice. Another example would be the prophesy concerning John the Baptist in Luke 1:15. It says he shall be filled with the Holy Spirit even from His mother's womb. How can you be filled with the Holy Spirit from your mother's womb if you are as the pro-abortionist say, not really a person?

Yes, the warfare for our children is on.

TIME OUT:

1.   Read the stories in Luke 1:44 and Luke 1:15.

2. Read the Christmas story in Luke 2 and notice the warfare King Herod had on children and especially the Christ child.

What We Can Learn From Christmas

In Luke 1:28, the angel said some things to Mary that I believe can benefit us in the day in which we live.

First, the angel said, "...Greetings, you who are highly favored. The Lord is with you." These words whispered nearly 2,000 years ago have great relevance today, if applied. We are highly favored people, because the Lord is with us.

As a matter of fact, Christmas is "Emmanuel," which means, "God with us!" We celebrate Christmas because God drew near to man by providing access to the Father and heaven by sending His Son to die on the cross. Thank God Jesus came, grew up, and chose to be obedient to the point of death. In doing so, He provided for us an atonement for sin. Hallelujah!

We are highly favored people because Jesus Christ is in our lives. Psalm 5:12 says, "For surely, O Lord, you bless the righteous; you surround them with your favor as with a shield." Favor comes from God. God can open doors that seem absolutely improbable because of His favor. His favor draws people to us, and in turn we are favored. He surrounds us with favor as a shield. There is a warmth, a drawing, a likableness to the people of God. This is all because of Jesus. It allows us to minister to others for the glory of God.

I wake up many mornings and claim God's favor in my day. I ask Jesus to give me favor with people and have them accept me so I may help build relationships for the Kingdom of God. I pray my phone calls, my letters, and my conversation are all blessed with His favor.

When Emmanuel is with you, you are highly favored as Mary was. The angel also said in verse 30 to not be afraid. These words are greatly needed in our society today with the increase of crime, gang violence, and other social ills. Peace is the greatest commodity needed in our world today. Jesus is the "Prince of Peace." Jesus is Emmanuel, God with us. He cancels the fear and brings the peace when He is in our lives.

Luke 1: 32-33 says the angel speaks something to Mary that absolutely thrills my heart. The angel states the excellency, the majesty, and permanency of Christ by saying His Kingdom will never end. Not in a thousand years, not in a million years, never! I have a friend who wrote a song entitled, Forever is a Long, Long, Time. It will be worth it all when we see Jesus. Life's trials will seem so small when we see Him. This life is so short compared to eternity. His Kingdom shall have no end.

TIME OUT:

1. Read the story of Mary and the angel in Luke 1:26-38.

2. Read Psalm 5:12, 1 John 4:18 and 2 Timothy 1:7.

11

ADULT BEHAVIOR VS. CHILDLIKE BEHAVIOR

Accepting Responsibility
Self Determination
Saying "No" Without Guilt
Confrontation Is Necessary
Ability to Compliment
Remaining Childlike:
Curiosity, Trusting, Wonder,
Innocence

ADULT BEHAVIOR VS. CHILDLIKE BEHAVIOR

Hebrews 5:12-14 says, "In fact, though by this time you ought to be teachers, you need someone to teach you the elementary truths of God's word all over again. You need milk, not solid food! Anyone who lives on milk, being still an infant, is not acquainted with the teaching about righteousness. But solid food is for the mature, who by constant use have trained themselves to distinguish good from evil."

These scriptures talk about being a "babe" or growing up. Two other verses that talk about maturity and adult behavior would be Colossians 1:28 and Romans 8:29. It is very evident in the Bible that we need to grow spiritually. Just as one grows physically, we also grow spiritually. Just as we start out as a child and become an adult physically, we do the same spiritually. We want to discuss in this chapter some signs of adult behavior as well as several areas where we need to remain childlike.

1 Corinthians 13:11 says, "When I was a child, I talked like a child, I thought like a child, I reasoned like a child. When I became a man, I put childish ways behind me." It is okay to be a child because we all need to start somewhere. Although, there comes a time when we need to do away with childish things.

Accepting Responsibility

It is childish behavior to constantly blame-shift. A sign of adult behavior is to take responsibility for your own actions. It is a sign of maturity to be able to say, "I messed up. I want to learn so I can correct the problem in case there is a next time." Adam and Eve blame-shifted in the garden. Adam quickly pointed out that it was the woman, and the woman tried to blame it on the serpent. No one wanted to say, "I messed up." It is amazing the number of times in a football game your players come to you on the sidelines after something went wrong, and you try to figure out how to correct it, yet no one is responsible. All five of the offensive linemen will say, "I got my man. I got my man. I got my man. I got my man. I got my man." As their coach, I have to say, "Then why did number 50 not get blocked? We will watch the films tomorrow, because the films won't lie. We'll find out who messed up. We will watch the video tape of the game." We must understand that there will ultimately be a video tape of our life when we stand before the Lord someday. We will have to take responsibility for our actions and attitudes then. We might as well do it now. When a player comes to the sideline and says, "I messed up, coach," you now have the ability to correct the mistake.

The same is true in our life. When we accept responsibility for our own actions, we can correct and make adjustments. If we always want to blame it on someone else, or on the circumstances, we will never be able to gain victory.

TIME OUT:

1.   Are you staying a babe in Christ, or are you growing up?

2.   Do you accept responsibility for your actions or do you blame-shift?

Self Determination

It is a sign of an adult to take control of our lives, and to use the skills, experiences, and education that we have to get a job and keep it. The Bible says if a man does not work, he shall not eat. People will pay you for your experience, skills and education, but we still have to motivate ourselves to keep that job by getting up each morning and doing the tasks our boss requires of us. I have seen person after person who cannot hold down a job. I believe this would be a sign of childish behavior. We need to learn to motivate ourselves. We need a determination about life. We need to determine to provide for our families. We need to determine to be the spiritual leader of our family. We need to be determined to reach our goals and dreams in life.

On athletic teams, a coach loves self-starters. He appreciates those who can motivate themselves and who are determined to be the best they can be without having to crack the whip all the time. Most people learn quickly in the real world that either you have the determination or you do not. No one is going to make you do anything. You have to do it for yourself. When you do, it is a sign of adult behavior.

TIME OUT:

1.   Are you self motivated or does someone else have to motivate you?

2.   Write down some of your goals and be determined to reach them.

Saying "NO" Without Guilt

Another sign of adult behavior is to say "no" without feeling guilty. Some people are not able to say "no" to anything. This is very childish because they try to fulfill everything they commit to and they end up driving themselves crazy or they end up breaking their commitments. This is because they "over-book" themselves. It is adult-like to be able to look at your schedule and prioritize the things you want to say "yes" to, and "no" to the things you do not want to do. When we say "no," we need to learn to say it without feeling guilty. It is the devil and other people who try to make us feel guilty when we say "no."

Too many times we let the priorities of others take precedence over what we feel God wants us to do. When we think about children, they have no idea what is important and what is not. They float on every whim. I hear my own children saying, "Let's do this." "Let's do that." They don't have much of a sense of priority. We should not feel guilty when we say "no" to our children. They may not seem to understand at the time, but a part of their character is being formed when we say "no."

It is hard for me to say "no." Too many times I try to please everyone, and I find I end up hurting the people I love the most. It is usually my kids and my wife who suffer when I do not say "no" often enough. Proverbs 29:25 says, "Fear of man will prove to be a snare, but whoever trusts in the Lord is kept safe." We cannot fear man and what he thinks of us when we say "no." We need to learn what God wants us to do and then go with Him.

TIME OUT:

1.   Do you try to please everyone?

2.   Read Galatians 1:10 and Proverbs 29:25.

Confrontation Is Necessary

Confrontation is not an easy part of being a Christian. No one really likes to do it, but it is still necessary to restore relationships that have somehow been severed. Most people wait until they are furious, and then they explode. We need to be able to tell someone when we have a problem that relates to them, and ask if they are willing to sit down and talk about it. We should be able to say, "Pastor So and So, something you said bothered me." It is a sign of adult behavior to confront one another. Instead of confronting, most people gossip. They would rather talk to someone else about their problems rather than go directly to the person involved. Gossiping is very childish behavior.

Additionally, we need to learn to confront in the correct manner. Approaching someone in anger and exploding, will never solve the problem. Ephesians 4:15 says that we are to "speak the truth in love." Proverbs 3:3 says, "Let love and faithfulness never leave you; bind them around your neck, write them on the tablet of your heart." We have to confront in love and kindness. It is usually best to do it right away rather than let something become a major issue.

Many times we do not even know when such a situation exists. When we become aware of a problem, we should deal with it immediately. The Bible says in 1 Thessalonians 5:13, "Hold them in the highest regard in love because of their work. Live in peace with each other." Confrontation should not be a negative term, but a positive one. It can help us live at peace with all men. We all try to avoid it, but if we can become skilled in confronting in a loving and kind manner, it will help us keep peace in our relationships.

TIME OUT:

1. Do you gossip? Do you confront others in love?

2. Read Ephesians 4:15 and Proverbs 3:3.

Ability To Compliment

The ability to compliment is another sign of adult behavior. We should learn to appreciate others and what they do. Jesus told us that if we give a cup of cold water in His name, He will be glorified. We should not be exclusively givers or takers. Being complimentary to others shows that we are secure enough in ourselves to let them know they are doing well. People who tear others down with their words are usually insecure people. They try to make themselves look better by making others look bad. That is why a sign of adult behavior is the ability to compliment. To say, "I like this or that about you," or "I appreciate what you have done," is a sign that you are thinking of others. Not only does it prove maturity and security in regards to ourselves, but compliments are healthy for the recipient as well.

On another note, there are those whose compliments do not come from a sincere heart. They are using flattery. Flattery is described in Webster's dictionary as, "excessive or insincere praise." Proverbs 26:28 says, "A lying tongue hates those it hurts, and a flattering mouth works ruin." Flattery is often used to manipulate. There is usually a selfish or insecure motive behind those who use flattery. Many times it is evident when someone is using flattery versus someone paying you a sincere compliment.

By complimenting, you can be doing more for others than you may think. Compliments can brighten a day as well as provide encouragement. The Bible says in Philippians 2:3-4, "Do nothing out of selfish ambition or vain conceit, but in humility consider others better than yourselves. Each of you should look not only to your own interests, but also to the interests of others." By being complimentary, we are looking out for the interest of others.

TIME OUT:

1. Read Philippians 2:3-4 and Hebrews 3:13.

2. Do you compliment others frequently?

Remaining Childlike

We have discussed signs of adult behavior, but there are some areas where we need to remain childlike. Notice I said "childlike," and not "childish." Childish would be when we are not acting like an adult. Childlike would be those characteristics of a child that Jesus wants us to have even as an adult.

Curiosity

We need to remain like a child in our curiosity. Have you noticed how many questions children ask? They ask questions like, "Why are bananas yellow?" and "Where did God come from?" My daughter, Carissa, asks a million questions. That is okay. Actually, that is good, because they are questions based on curiosity. We need to keep our curiosity about the things of God and life. That is how we learn.

I do not believe God is intimidated in the least to have us question Him. I heard the story about George Washington Carver who one time approached God and said, "Why did you make the sky blue?" God somehow impressed upon him that it was too big of a question for him. Then he came back to God and asked, "Why did you make me?" God said, "That is still too big of a question for you." The same boy was kicking his foot on the ground and came across some peanuts. He asked God, "Why did you make peanuts?" God came back and said, "Now that's a good question." The story goes on to tell how George Washington Carver invented hundreds of ways to use peanuts. That's what curiosity does. We need to remain childlike in our curiosity. We will never discover the things God wants us to discover without curiosity.

Trusting

We also are to remain childlike in our trust. Our society is such that we do not trust anyone anymore. Children trust everyone. My daughter answered the door one day while my wife was upstairs taking a shower. Being a little child, she just opened the door in a very trusting manner even though there was a stranger on the other side. This just shows the trust of a little child. Many times, this kind of situation can turn into a negative one. We, as adults, have to teach them not to trust certain people. We teach them not to speak to strangers, that all of life is not fair, and sometimes people will let you down. But we need to make sure that we do not become cynical. Remember the trust of a child and you will be reminded to trust others and believe in people.

I heard the story of Nicky Cruz, a former gang leader in New York City. David Wilkerson was holding some meetings where many of the gang members attended. Some of the gang members were asked to take up the offering. The building was designed in such a way that after they had collected the money, they had to go outside first before returning with the money. Many of those gang members wanted to take off with the offering. Nicky Cruz said, "No, we are taking all of it to the front. This is the first time in my life that anyone has ever trusted me with anything." It was this trust that brought him to Jesus Christ.

We need to rekindle the trust of a little child within ourselves. Be vulnerable and trust people until they give us a reason not to. I am not saying to trust people who have proven themselves not trustworthy, but we need to give people a chance. We need to give them a second chance. I like the statement one pastor made in regards to being in the ministry. He said, "Those who want to be used of God, get used." There are going to be times when people take advantage of us and even rip us off. We still have to take a chance with people. It is still worth it to reach that one, even if others somehow take advantage of us.

Wonder

We also need to remain childlike in our excitement and our wonder about life. Isn't it exciting to watch young ones at Christmas? They become so excited about the presents and putting up the tree. Many times, as adults, we can become cynical or apathetic. My wife and I have joked about the stress of the holidays. We say, "This is the time I hate the best." We cannot let ourselves go this direction. Children get excited about God. They want to learn more about what He says, how He operates and how He affects our lives. We need to rekindle some of our youthfulness in the way we approach life. We cannot lose our excitement, our zeal and our wonder.

Innocence

Finally, never lose your innocence. Some people feel that children need to grow up quickly and learn how the world works. I happen to disagree. What happened to the old values and morals? We are losing them. They are being pushed aside and written off as "old fashioned." Our country was founded on godly values and godly standards. They are slowly slipping away, and it is a terrifying thing. The more we can shield our children from the filth and perversion, the better. Children do not know about many things until they are exposed to them. It should be the same with us. The Bible says in Matthew 5:8, "Blessed are the pure in heart, for they will see God." Proverbs 15:26 says, "The Lord detests the thoughts of the wicked, but those of the pure are pleasing to him." We should try to keep our thoughts and actions innocent by not exposing ourselves to the perverseness on television, magazines, and other forms of media and, most importantly, by cleansing our minds through the reading and studying of God's Word.

TIME OUT:

1.   Commit to remaining childlike in your trust, wonder, curiosity, and innocence.

2.   Which one of these topics do you need to nurture the most?

12

How to
be an
Overcomer

Warrior Spirit
Use What God Gives You
Full of Faith
Men Full of Heart and Soul
Complete the Job
Jonathan Tasted the Sweetness of Victory

Warrior Spirit

If we are going to be an overcomer, we must possess a warrior spirit. 1 Samuel 14:1 tells of the day Jonathan, the son of Saul, said to the young man bearing his armor, "Come, let's go over to the Philistine outpost on the other side." Jonathan possessed a warrior's spirit. The presence of the enemy in our life should rouse our courage. It definitely roused Jonathan's courage. Again, in 1 Samuel 14:6, Jonathan said, "Come, let's go over to the outpost of those uncircumcised fellows." Wouldn't it be absurd for Jonathan to sit back while the rest of the raiding parties went out? Wouldn't it be equally absurd for us to sit back as we see the enemy taking hold of our country and world as he has? Shouldn't our courage be roused also?

Consider some of these statistics. Fifteen percent of all young people under 18 years old have serious mental and emotional problems. Out of 29 million teenagers, 500,000 will attempt suicide this year; 10 percent will succeed. One million will run away from home, and 250,000 teenage girls will give birth to illegitimate babies. 378,000 teenagers will receive an abortion, and over three million have a serious drinking problem. Four million children will be beaten, molested, or otherwise abused by their parents. One out of every four women has been abused or sexually assaulted by some man in their girlhood. Sixty-five percent of 12- to 17-year olds have tried alcohol and even a higher rate for 25-year olds, with a rate of 94 percent. Out of 2,487,000 marriages, there are 1,155,000 divorces.

Now those statistics do one of two things to you. They either cause you to give up hope, or rouse the warrior spirit in you. It either makes you say, "What's the use." or it makes you roll up your sleeves and get busy, knowing that God is able to do anything. There is NOTHING too hard for God.

David had a warrior spirit. In 1 Samuel 17:32-37 he told Saul he would fight Goliath. Verse 32 says, "...Let no one lose heart on account of this Philistine; your servant will go and fight him." In verse 33 Saul said, "…'You are not able to go out against this Philistine and fight him; you are only a boy, and he has been a fighting man from his youth.'" Then in verses 34 and 35, David said to Saul, "…'Your servant has been keeping his father's sheep. When a lion or a bear came and carried off a sheep from the flock, I went after it, struck it and rescued the sheep from its mouth. When it turned on me, I seized it by its hair, struck at and killed it.'" Verse 36 says, "Your servant has killed both the lion and the bear; this uncircumcised Philistine will be like one of them, because he has defied the armies of the living God."

Verse 37 says, "The Lord who delivered me from the paw of the lion and the paw of the bear will deliver me from the hand of this Philistine." It was Goliath mocking God that incited David's fury. It aroused the warrior spirit that was in David. When we see the incidents going on in our world today that are basically mocking God. It ought to arouse the warrior spirit in us enough so that we do something about it.

Peter had a warrior spirit. It was this warrior spirit in Peter that had him proclaiming the gospel in Acts 2:36-40.

Paul was also a man who possessed a warrior spirit. The man who once persecuted Christians and put them to death now used his energies and warrior spirit to proclaim the gospel. In 1 Corinthians 9:26-27 he said, "Therefore I do not run like a man running aimlessly; I do not fight like a man beating the air. No, I beat my body and make it my slave so that after I have preached to others, I myself will not be disqualified for the prize." Paul lived in the trenches. He looked at his imprisonment as a chance to preach to kings. He looked at his death as a final victory and a chance to see Jesus. He was also the one who said in Philippians 1:21, "For to me, to live is Christ and to die is gain." Those who possess a warrior spirit give their all to see lives changed and see God glorified.

TIME OUT:

1.   Do you have a warrior spirit or a coward spirit?

2.   Read 1 Samuel 17:32-34 and 1 Samuel 14.

3.   In what areas of your life do you need to overcome?

Use What God Gives You

Jonathan knew that the best defense was a good offense. Isn't that true in football? When you know the other team has a great offense, you want to keep them off the field. The best way to do that is by controlling the ball and keeping your offense on the field. That was true of the New York Giants when they beat the Buffalo Bills 20 to 19 in Super Bowl XXV. The only chance the Giants had were to run the ball and keep the Bills' offense off the field. Jonathan was a man who would rather die trying than to sit around in defeat. Those who sit around and never try are already failures, for they have let the fear of failure keep them from getting in the battle.

Jonathan said in 1 Samuel 14:6, "...Perhaps the Lord will act on our behalf...." Jonathan knew that those who sit around doing nothing for God will eventually be found and disposed of by the enemy. You may say, "I don't have this" or "I'm not good at that." Stop looking at what you do not have, and use what you do have. David only had a slingshot and a few stones, but he used what God gave him.

Peter only had a testimony. He did not know that much about God's Word, but Peter had experienced Jesus Christ. He had experienced the Holy Spirit. Peter knew what he used to be, and he knew what God had made him into now. He knew the difference in his life. Peter also knew a few scriptures. Peter used what he had when he started preaching on the Day of Pentecost in Acts 2:14-41. When Peter and John were commanded not to preach in the name of Jesus in Acts 4:19-20, again Peter used what he had. He used his testimony. He said, "Whether it is right in the sight of God to give heed to you rather than to God, you be the judge, for we cannot stop speaking of what we have seen and heard." All Peter did was speak on what he had seen, heard, and how it changed his life. If we are going to be overcomers, we are going to have to use what God has given us. We will not only be overcomers, but we will help others overcome as well.

What are some of the offensive weapons God has given to us? Revelation 12:11 says, "They overcame him by the blood of the Lamb and the Word of their testimony...." Testimony is one of the offensive weapons God has given to us. No one can dispute your testimony. No one can dispute what happened to you. Because of what Jesus Christ did by shedding His blood, and the effect it has had on your life by receiving Jesus Christ, your testimony is very powerful. No one can argue when you say, "This is what happened to me. This is what Jesus has done in my life." It is a weapon to be used. It does not have to be used in a belligerent, arrogant or cocky fashion, but it is a way of giving praise and glory to God. Sharing your testimony can help others overcome, but it can also help you overcome. It reminds you of what God has done in your life and even though you may not have the gospel outline memorized, it will remind you of what Jesus Christ has done in your life.

You have a story to tell. It brings glory to God. It brings a separation from the world and leaves people hungry, knowing there is something better for them. People are always looking for something better and for a happier life. That is why all the commercials, especially the beer commercials, appeal to the people to live for the moment by saying, "If you don't deserve it, who does?" "Have it your way." But people are looking for something more, and they deserve to have the answer. Your testimony is a part of that answer to help them overcome. 1 Peter 3:15 says, "...Always be prepared to give an answer to everyone who asks you to give the reason for the hope that you have. But do this with gentleness and respect...." We do not have to shove the gospel down anyone's throat. We can share our testimony gently and respectfully.

Another weapon we have is prayer. Prayer is an offensive weapon that God wants us to use to not only overcome in our life, but also help others overcome. James 5:16 says, "...The effectual fervent prayer of a righteous man availeth much (KJV)." Notice that it is not any old prayer, it is the "the effectual fervent prayer." We need to realize we are battling for ourselves and others when we go to prayer. We should not say our prayers haphazardly. We are battling for the souls of men. We need to understand that there is a war going on.

The Bible says in James 5:17-18, "Elijah was a man just like us. He prayed earnestly that it would not rain, and it did not rain on the land for three and a half years. Again he prayed and the heavens gave rain..." Elijah was a man just like us. The Bible is saying that our prayers can have the same kind of effect as Elijah's had. Prayer is one of our offensive weapons that must be used if we are to overcome and help others to overcome.

We also have the weapon of praise. Hebrews 13:15 says, "Through Jesus, therefore, let us continually offer to God a sacrifice of praise–the fruit of lips that confess his name." It says to do this continually, and it is to be a sacrifice of praise. That means we are to do it even when we don't feel like doing it. The Bible says God inhabits the praises of His people. God comes in a very special way when people give praise to His name. 2 Chronicles 20:22 says, "As they began to sing and praise, the Lord set ambushes against the men of Ammon and Moab and Mount Seir who were invading Judah, and they were defeated." Notice this happened when they began to sing and praise God.

In Matthew, the Bible declares that if we fail to praise Him, the rocks will cry out. If we want to see people free in Jesus Christ, we need to be in an atmosphere where we can draw close to God. Praise is where we can draw close to God. James 4:7-8 says, "Submit yourselves, then, to God. Resist the devil, and he will flee from you. Come near to God and he will come near to you..." Too many times it is our sophistication and our worry about what other people think about us that keeps us from praising and honoring

God with our worship. One of the most liberating things we can do in our lives that will help us overcome on a daily basis, is to learn to praise Him in the many different ways the Bible talks about; for instance, clapping our hands, raising our hands, sitting alone quietly, singing to Him, praising and shouting His name. Different situations call for different things and different kinds of praise.

The final offensive weapon I would like to discuss that can help us be an overcomer is the Word of God. Hebrews 4:12 says, "For the word of God is living and active. Sharper than any double-edged sword, it penetrates even to dividing soul and spirit, joints and marrow; it judges the thoughts and attitudes of the heart." The Word of God divides soul and spirit. God has a way of putting his finger on different areas of our life to show us where we need to change. I do not believe anyone can become an overcomer unless they know the Word of God. There is nothing more essential to the Christian life than the Word of God. We need daily doses of the Word of God if we are going to live right and be all Jesus intended us to be.

It is the Word of God that will keep us on track and point out the error of our ways when we leave that straight and narrow path. Romans 10:17 says, "...faith comes by hearing the message, and the message is heard through the Word of Christ." Our faith is built up by the Word of God. 1 Peter 2:2 says, "...Crave pure spiritual milk, so that by it you may grow up in your salvation." We cannot grow and mature as a Christian without the Word of God.

TIME OUT:

1. Are you using your talent, money and time for God?

2. Are you using all your spiritual weapons?

Full of Faith

If we are going to be overcomers, we need to be people of faith. We need to be full of faith. In our story of Jonathan and his armor-bearer, 1 Samuel 14:6 says, "...Nothing can hinder the Lord from saving, whether by many or by few." Jesus said, "If you have faith as a mustard seed, you shall say to this mountain to be removed and it will be cast into the sea." A little faith can produce a great victory! It is God's desire to increase our faith and to bring us to a place where we are like Jonathan. A place where we take the limits off the Lord and we know He can save by many or by few. As a matter of fact, when He brings the victory by few rather than by many, God gets all of the glory. Often men get the glory when God saves by many.

When Jesus raised Lazarus from the dead, His desire was to increase their faith and to take them from glory to glory. They had believed that Jesus was the healer, but what about Jesus as the one who had victory over death? Jesus wanted to prove that He had victory over death itself. When Jesus heard Lazarus was sick, He stayed where He was two more days. He did not do this to be cruel. He said in John 11:15, "and for your sake I am glad that I was not there, so that you may believe...." God wants to keep increasing our faith where we don't limit God.

Jonathan's faith led him to his hands and knees. Jonathan and his armor-bearer had already consulted the Lord in prayer, but in 1 Samuel 14:12, the men of the outpost shouted to Jonathan and his armor-bearer, "Come up to us and we will teach you a lesson." So Jonathan said to his armor-bearer, "Climb up after me." The Lord had given them into the hand of Israel. Jonathan climbed up using his hands and feet with his armor-bearer behind him. The Philistines fell before Jonathan. His armor-bearer followed, killing men behind him. The Philistine army was facing double trouble. They messed with Jonathan and his armor-bearer when they were full of faith in God. Notice that they sought the Lord before they went into action.

TIME OUT:

1. Do you have faith that God will help you overcome every problem and situation in your life?

2. Read 1 Samuel 14:6-28.

Men Full of Heart and Soul

We need to put men next to ourselves who are full of heart and soul as Jonathan did. Jonathan's armor-bearer was full of heart and soul. Heart, meaning faith and passion. Soul, meaning he was committed to Jonathan and was willing to let Jonathan take the lead while he followed. He was his soul-mate. In 1 Samuel 14:7 Jonathan's armor-bearer says, "Go ahead; I am with you heart and soul." In other words, whatever you want me to do, I'll do it. I believe in you and I am willing to win or lose with you. We have fought enough battles in the past and I trust you.

In 2 Samuel 23:8, David spoke of some of the mighty men he had surrounded himself with. He spoke of Josheb-Basshebeth, who killed 800 men in one encounter with a spear. He spoke of Eleazar, who with David in 2 Samuel 23:10 said his hand grew tired and froze to the sword. The Lord brought a great victory that day. In 2 Samuel 23:18, David spoke of Abishai, the brother of Joab, who raised his spear against 300 men whom he killed.

Finally, 2 Samuel 23:20 speaks of Benaiah who struck down two of Moab's best men and killed a lion in a pit on a snowy day. It calls him a "valiant fighter who performed great exploits." He also struck down a huge Egyptian. Although the Egyptian had a spear in his hand, Benaiah went against him with a club. He snatched the spear from the Egyptian's hand and killed him with his own spear. If we are going to be overcomers, we need to surround ourselves with people of courage, people of loyalty, and people who are with us heart and soul.

The people we surround ourselves with should supply:

Accountability. The Bible says as iron sharpens iron, one man sharpens another. I believe this is one of the greatest reasons Promise Keepers has taken off as it has. It is causing men to keep their commitments by being accountable to one another. People who are willing to confront one another, while loving one another. People who are willing to accept one another, but at the same time, not approve of everything going on in their life and be willing to talk about those areas. Men need people who will keep them accountable for various decisions in their life. We all need it.

Because of the encouragement we need, these people should also be full of heart and soul. I have heard it said before that friendship doubles the joy and divides the sorrow. When we face various trials in our life, we need someone to bear that burden with us. We also need someone to encourage us. The Bible says "But encourage one another daily, as long as it is called Today, so that none of you may be hardened by sin's deceitfulness" (Hebrews 3:13). Notice the word "courage" is in the middle of "encouragement." We gain a greater courage to do things for God. We attempt things for God we may not think are possible when we have someone rooting for us. We need men next to us who will be encouragers as well as someone who will keep us accountable.

We also need men around us because of the strength factor it provides. Ecclesiastes 4:11-12 says, "Also, if two lie down together, they will keep warm. But how can one keep warm alone? Though one may be overpowered, two can defend themselves. A cord of three strands is not quickly broken." The Bible says one will put a thousand to flight and two will put ten thousand to flight. There is a greater strength when people walk together. Amos 3:3 says, "Do two walk together unless they have agreed to do so?" There is strength in agreement. When someone agrees before God in prayer, there is a strength and a power there. Matthew 18:19 says, "Again, I tell you that if two of you on earth agree about anything you ask for, it will be done for you by my Father in heaven." There is a greater power when we have men next to us who are with us heart and soul.

Complete the Job

1 Samuel 14:13 says, "…The Philistines fell before Jonathan, and his armor-bearer followed and killed behind him…" They were there to finish a job. The job was not completed until the Philistines were finished off. Although the Philistines fell down before Jonathan, the job was not completed until the armor-bearer followed and finished the job. If we are going to be an overcomer, we will have to finish the job and complete what God has started. Doesn't it really bother you when people do something in a half-way fashion? People constantly try to do things in a mediocre way. They do them, but they do not do them well. We need to be disciplined enough to not only finish the job, but to do our best job. The past two seasons at Phoenix Christian High School, where I coach, we have gone 9-0 in the regular season, but then we won only one playoff game. We did not complete the job. We ended both seasons with a 10-1 record. Most people might be excited about going 10-1, but we were not because we did not finish the job. We have some unfinished business to take care of in the years to come.

TIME OUT:

1. Make sure to complete each task God has given you. Do not settle for "good enough."

2. Write down some of the areas you lack completion and concentrate on completing them.

3. Do you have people in your life that are with you heart and soul? Do they bring some accountability and encouragement?

Jonathan Tasted the Sweetness of Victory

One of the great joys about being an overcomer, is to look back on the things you have defeated in your life. There is great joy and a real sweetness on the other end of our battles. Most people say, after they have gone through a major trial or problem, that they never want to go through it again. Although, they are glad they had the experience because of all the lessons they learned. That is "the sweetness" we are speaking of. After all the hard work on an athletic field, all the wind sprints, all the practice, the preparation, when you reach the end of those battles and come out victorious, how sweet it is.

In 1 Samuel 14:27, Jonathan eats the honey that was forbidden to others. Jonathan was in the battle while Saul only started programs. The entire army of Israel had been in the battle, but only Jonathan was refreshed in the end. In 1 Samuel 14:24, it says, "Now the men of Israel were in distress that day, because Saul had bound the people under an oath, saying, 'Cursed be any man who eats food before evening comes, before I have avenged myself on my enemies!' So none of the troops tasted food." Jonathan did not know of the food being forbidden for others so he was refreshed. If we are busy doing what God desires for us, we won't have time to become bound to legalism. I have heard it said before that if we stay busy in the battle, we won't have time to do the things God would not have us do. One man said, "If you spend your time doing the do's, you won't have time to do the don'ts." We need to stay in the battle. We need to overcome for our families and for our neighborhoods and for people who are in need of Jesus Christ. You can taste the sweetness of victory in your own life, but it is even greater when you help others overcome and taste the sweetness of victory.

I love the quote Joe Paterno gave in the 1973 Commencement Address at Penn State. He said, "We strive to be No. 1. We work hard to achieve our goals. When Saturday comes, we will walk on the grass in this stadium, and stand as a team. We tighten up our belts, we look across at our opponents, we say, 'Come on, let's go. Let's see how good you are. Let's play.' We play with enthusiasm and recklessness. We are not afraid to lose." This sums up the spirit of an overcomer.

TIME OUT:

1.   Have you overcome in some areas? Write them down.

2.   You can only gain the victory if you do not fear defeat, but trust God!

13

SCRIPTURE MEMORY

Salvation and Important Truths
The Word
Love and Dealing with People
Humility

SCRIPTURE MEMORY

The single most useful discipline that has helped me grow as a Christian, is scripture memory. There was a time when I devoted many years to scripture memorization.

The benefit of having the Word of God deep down in your heart and ready in your mind is truly amazing. We know that Jesus quoted the Word when He was tempted by the devil. I know the Lord brings these scriptures to our remembrance when we need them in the spiritual battle we are involved in daily. He brings scriptures to mind that we need at that particular time or for that particular circumstance. Scripture memorization also helps in giving a defense for our faith and supports others in their spiritual pilgrimage.

I have included a few of the scriptures we used with the Phoenix Suns and Arizona Cardinals. It has been very encouraging to watch members of both teams get excited about memorizing scripture. We would memorize one or two a week, and they were expected to quote them at the next chapel in front of their teammates who were present. I watched some who thought they could not do it–do it, and love it. You will also, if you will take three by five cards and write down the scriptures you like. I suggest some of the ones on the Word of God and salvation at first. I have also included some scriptures on humility and love. Walk your neighborhood or around the house going through those three by five cards several times a week. Start with two or three a week until you get up to around 20 cards. Then just add one or two a week. I eventually created three categories. The scriptures I knew well, the ones I did not know well, and the ones that I needed to learn because they had very important truths in them.

I promise it will be a great benefit to your walk with Christ!

Salvation and Important Truths

JOHN 1:12

Yet to all who received him, to those who believed in his name, he gave the right to become children of God.

JOHN 16:24

Until now you have not asked for anything in my name. Ask and you will receive, and your joy will be complete.

MATTHEW 6:33

But seek first his kingdom and his righteousness, and all these things will be given to you as well.

1 JOHN 1:9

If we confess our sins, he is faithful and just and will forgive us our sins and purify us from all unrighteousness.

EPHESIANS 3:20

Now to him who is able to do immeasurably more than all we ask or imagine, according to his power that is at work within us.

EPHESIANS 2:8-9

For it is by grace you have been saved, through faith–and this is not from yourselves, it is the gift of God–not by works, so that no one can boast.

ROMANS 1:16

I am not ashamed of the gospel, because it is the power of God for the salvation of everyone who believes: first for the Jew, then for the Gentile.

PHILIPPIANS 1:6

> Being confident of this, he who began a good work in you will carry it on to completion until the day of Christ Jesus.

ROMANS 10:9-10

> That if you confess with your mouth, "Jesus as Lord," and believe in your heart that God raised Him from the dead, you will be saved. For it is with your heart that you believe and are justified, and it is with your mouth that you confess and are saved.

2 CORINTHIANS 5:17

> Therefore, if anyone is in Christ, he is a new creation; the old has gone, the new has come!

2 CORINTHIANS 5:21

> God made him who had no sin to be sin for us, so that in him we might become the righteousness of God.

The Word

1 PETER 2:2

> Like newborn babies, crave pure spiritual milk, so that by it you may grow up in your salvation.

HEBREWS 4:12

> For the word of God is living and active. Sharper than any double-edged sword, it penetrates even to dividing soul and spirit, joints and marrow; it judges the thoughts and attitudes of the heart.

2 TIMOTHY 3:16-17

> All Scripture is God-breathed and is useful for teaching, rebuking, correcting and training in righteousness, so that

the man of God may be thoroughly equipped for every good work.

2 TIMOTHY 2:15

Do your best to present yourself to God as one approved, a workman who does not need to be ashamed and who correctly handles the word of truth.

PSALM 119:11

I have hidden your word in my heart that I might not sin against you.

ROMANS 10:17

Consequently, faith comes from hearing the message, and the message is heard through the word of Christ.

Love and Dealing with People

JOHN 13:35

By this all men will know that you are my disciples, if you love one another.

JOHN 15:12

My command is this: Love each other as I have loved you.

ROMANS 12:10

Be devoted to one another in brotherly love. Honor one another above yourselves.

ROMANS 14:13

Therefore let us stop passing judgment on one another. Instead, make up your mind not to put any stumbling block or obstacle in your brother's way.

ROMANS 14:19

> Let us therefore make every effort to do what leads to peace and to mutual edification.

ROMANS 15:7

> Accept one another, then, just as Christ accepted you, in order to bring praise to God.

GALATIANS 5:13

> You, my brothers, were called to be free. But do not use your freedom to indulge the sinful nature; rather, serve one another in love.

GALATIANS 5:15

> If you keep on biting and devouring each other, watch out or you will be destroyed by each other.

GALATIANS 5:26

> Let us not become conceited, provoking and envying each other.

EPHESIANS 4:2

> Be completely humble and gentle; be patient, bearing with one another in love.

EPHESIANS 4:25

> Therefore each of you must put off falsehood and speak truthfully to his neighbor, for we are all members of one body.

EPHESIANS 4:32

> Be kind and compassionate to one another, forgiving each other, just as in Christ God forgave you.

EPHESIANS 5:19

Speak to one another with psalms, hymns and spiritual songs. Sing and make music in your heart to the Lord.

PHILIPPIANS 2:3

Do nothing out of selfish ambition or vain conceit, but in humility consider others better than yourselves.

COLOSSIANS 3:9

Do not lie to each other, since you have taken off your old self with its practices.

COLOSSIANS 3:13

Bear with each other and forgive whatever grievances you may have against one another. Forgive as the Lord forgave you.

COLOSSIANS 3:16

Let the word of Christ dwell in you richly as you teach and admonish one another with all wisdom, and as you sing psalms, hymns and spiritual songs with gratitude in your heart to God.

1 THESSALONIANS 3:12

May the Lord make your love increase and overflow for each other and for everyone else, just as ours does for you.

1 THESSALONIANS 4:18

Therefore encourage each other with these words.

1 THESSALONIANS 5:11

Therefore encourage one another and build each other up, just as in fact you are doing.

1 THESSALONIANS 5:13

Hold them in the highest regard in love because of their work. Live in peace with each other.

1 THESSALONIANS 5:15

Make sure that nobody pays back wrong for wrong, but always try to be kind to each other and to everyone else.

HEBREWS 3:13

But encourage one another daily, as long as it is called Today, so that none of you may be hardened by sin's deceitfulness.

HEBREWS 10:24

And let us consider how we may spur one another on toward love and good deeds.

JAMES 4:11

Brothers, do not slander one another. Anyone who speaks against his brother or judges him speaks against the law and judges it. When you judge the law, you are not keeping it, but sitting in judgment on it.

JAMES 5:9

Don't grumble against each other, brothers, or you will be judged. The Judge is standing at the door!

JAMES 5:16

Therefore, confess your sins to each other and pray for each other, so that you may be healed. The prayer of a righteous man is powerful and effective.

JAMES 3:17

But the wisdom that comes from heaven is first of all pure; then peace-loving, considerate, submissive, full of mercy and good fruit, impartial and sincere.

1 PETER 1:22

Now that you have purified yourselves by obeying the truth so that you have sincere love for your brothers, love one another deeply, from the heart.

1 PETER 4:9

Offer hospitality to one another without grumbling.

1 PETER 4:10

Each one should use whatever gift he has received to serve others, faithfully administering God's grace in its various forms.

1 JOHN 4:11

Dear friends, since God so loved us, we also ought to love one another.

Humility

PROVERBS 15:33

The fear of the Lord teaches a man wisdom, and humility comes before honor.

PROVERBS 16:18-19

Pride goes before destruction, and a haughty spirit before a fall. Better to be lowly in spirit and among the oppressed than to share plunder with the proud.

PROVERBS 18:12

Before his downfall a man's heart is proud, but humility comes before honor.

PROVERBS 25:6-7

Do not exalt yourself in the king's presence, and do not claim a place among great men; it is better for him to say to you, "Come up here."

PROVERBS 27:2

> Let another praise you, and not your own mouth; someone else, and not your own lips.

PROVERBS 30:32

> If you have played the fool and exalted yourself, or if you have planned evil, clap your hand over your mouth!

MICAH 6:8

> He has showed you, O man, what is good. And what does the Lord require of you? To act justly and to love mercy and to walk humbly with your God.

MARK 10:45

> For even the Son of Man did not come to be served, but to serve, and to give his life a ransom for many.

LUKE 14:8-11

> When someone invites you to a wedding feast, do not take the place of honor, for a person more distinguished than you may have been invited. If so, the host who invited both of you will come and say to you, "Give this man your seat." Then, humiliated, you will have to take the least important place. But when you are invited, take the lowest place, so that when your host comes, he will say to you, "Friend, move up to a better place." Then you will be honored in the presence of all your fellow guests. For everyone who exalts himself will be humbled, and he who humbles himself will be exalted.

JOHN 13:14

> Now that I, your Lord and Teacher, have washed your feet, you also should wash one another's feet.

2 CORINTHIANS 20:12

We do not dare to classify or compare ourselves with some who commend themselves. When they measure themselves by themselves and compare themselves with themselves, they are not wise.

PHILIPPIANS 2:3-4

Do nothing out of selfish ambition or vain conceit, but in humility consider others better than yourselves. Each of you should look not only to your own interests, but also to the interests of others.

PHILIPPIANS 3:12-14

Not that I have already obtained all this, or have already been made perfect, but I press on to take hold of that for which Christ Jesus took hold of me. Brothers, I do not consider myself yet to have taken hold of it. But one thing I do: Forgetting what is behind and straining toward what is ahead, I press on toward the goal to win the prize for which God has called me heavenward in Christ Jesus.